Aegean Legacies: Greek Island Embroideries from the
Ashmolean Museum

Published in the United Kingdom by Hali Publications Ltd.,
7 Ability Plaza, Arbutus Street, E8 4DT London
www.hali.com

Produced in collaboration with the Ashmolean Museum,
University of Oxford

Edited by Ben Evans, Brian David and Malin Lonnberg
Designed by Dorota Bojarovic

Printed in Latvia

British Library Cataloguing-in-Publication Data:
A catalogue record for this book is available from
the British Library

ISBN 9781898113973

Aegean Legacies

GREEK ISLAND EMBROIDERIES FROM THE ASHMOLEAN MUSEUM

Francesca Leoni

with contributions
by Susan Stanton

ASHMOLEAN MUSEUM OXFORD

HPL

Contents

Acknowledgements

A book is hardly ever the achievement of a single individual and this is especially so for the present catalogue, written during the lockdown caused by the Covid-19 pandemic.

The Keeper of the Eastern Art Department at the Ashmolean Museum, Dr Mallica Kumbera Landrus, endorsed the idea of a book on our Greek island embroideries from the start, encouraging and facilitating its delivery in more ways than one. Ben Evans, editor-in-chief at Hali Publications Ltd., accepted the challenge of publishing it, offering experienced professional support and securing financial backing. The contributions of Richard and Adeela de Unger, Bruce P. and Olive W. Baganz, Alastair and Kathy Dunn, Michael and Jacqueline Franses and Marshall and Marilyn R. Wolf have enabled us to bring it to fruition. I am especially grateful to them for their generosity, trust and encouragement without which we simply would not have been able to proceed.

My dear colleague Susan Stanton, textile conservator at the Ashmolean Museum, also deserves my sincerest thanks; it was she who taught me how to look at embroideries, and she contributed so much of the information offered here. The same goes for the expert advice of Penny Oakley, who enriched the catalogue with valuable insights. At the Ashmolean Museum and the University of Oxford, several other colleagues deserve mention and gratitude: Declan McCarthy, Sally Crawford, David Gowers, Anne Holly, Sibyl Searle, Amy Taylor, Katharina Ulmschneider and Adele West.

Across the country a number of scholars, curators and collection managers helped me piece together information about the embroidery collections in their care: Helen Ritchie at the Fitzwilliam Museum, University of Cambridge; Jill Winder and Rebecca Higgins at the Leeds University Museum; Pauline Rushton at the Liverpool Museum; Helen Wyld and Karen Johnston at the National Museums of Scotland, Edinburgh; Bill Griffiths and Kelly Martin at the Tyne & Wear Museum, Newcastle; and Ann French and Uthra Rajgopal at the Whitworth Gallery, University of Manchester. Their efforts and generosity during the challenging months of the first Covid-19 lockdown have been particularly appreciated. The additional help and feedback received from Ann French, Xenia Politou and Mariam Rosser-Owen also deserve thanks.

Last, but not least, I would like to express my sincerest gratitude to the whole team at Hali Publications Ltd., and in particular Malin Lonnberg. Malin's steady stewardship, efficient project managing and good humour made the whole experience very enjoyable in spite of the many challenges faced in the process.

This volume is dedicated to the late Marianne Ellis, a passionate embroidery specialist whose legacy at the Ashmolean Museum continues to be cherished.

Francesca Leoni

This catalogue was published in conjunction with the exhibition 'Mediterranean Threads: 18th- and 19th-Century Greek Embroideries' held at the Ashmolean Museum, University of Oxford, between 12 September 2020 and 6 June 2021

Foreword

The Ashmolean Museum in Oxford is home to many wonders, including one of the most fascinating and eclectic textile collections in the UK. The pieces range from ancient Egyptian and Coptic textiles to Gujarati printed cottons, via 17th-century English embroideries, offering countless avenues for investigation and exploration.

Highly valued and highly portable, textiles have often been vehicles of cultural exchange and agents of influence. This is amply demonstrated through this catalogue, which presents a selection of our modern Greek island embroidery collection. The cross-cultural conversations that can be unpicked from these textiles form the focus of this book; the same can be said of the Museum's exhibition that gave rise to it: 'Mediterranean Threads: 18th- and 19th-Century Greek Embroideries' (12 September 2020–6 June 2021).

These island textiles shed light on Britain's enduring fascination for Greek culture, reflected in the nature of much of the Ashmolean's collection. This book explores these complex threads and suggests many fertile areas for research that these and related Ashmolean textiles present. In this context we look forward to the creation in the months ahead of a new textile research centre that will bring together the Ashmolean's collections with the equally opulent and complementary holdings of the Pitt Rivers Museum. This will, we hope, unlock the extraordinarily rich potential of these collections for further teaching and study.

We are, as ever, sincerely grateful to the various supporters of this volume – Richard and Adeela de Unger, Bruce P. and Olive W. Baganz, Alastair and Kathy Dunn, Michael and Jacqueline Franses and Marshall and Marilyn R. Wolf – for their generosity and interest in the project. We also thank Hali Publications Ltd, its editors and staff, for taking on the task of producing such a handsome and beautifully illustrated volume.

Xa Sturgis

PART I

GREEK ISLAND EMBROIDERIES: AN OVERVIEW

Introduction

Anyone unfamiliar with the history and traditions of Greek island embroideries might expect to find a cohesive group of textiles, sharing both style and formal characteristics, in a book dedicated to the subject. However, just a quick look through these pages is enough to realise that diversity is their primary common denominator. Although comparatively smaller than those available in other public institutions around the country and abroad,[1] the collection of the Ashmolean Museum of Art and Archaeology, University of Oxford, contains enough material to highlight the stylistic and technical range of embroideries from islands that are sometimes only a short distance apart. This catalogue is an opportunity to introduce this little-known collection through a selection of twenty-five examples datable between the 17th and the 19th century.[2]

The focus on insular rather than mainland products reflects the nature of the Ashmolean's holdings and the greater attention paid to the former category by their collectors, who were possibly attracted by their richer colouring and more elaborate designs. As such, this book does not offer a comprehensive survey of the whole Greek embroidery tradition, but rather aims to contribute fresh evidence and perspectives in relation to the textiles linked to the Greek archipelago.[3]

The Greek embroideries in the Ashmolean Museum include fragments of cushion covers, pillowcases, bed valances, tents and curtains, as well as items of dress. The majority were donated between 1960 and 1978 by Professor John Linton Myres and John Buxton, two individuals with Oxford connections (**Figs. 1–2**). The embroideries from Myres would appear to be only a portion of his original collection, however. Their limited range and fragmentary nature, in fact, contrast with the observations about their quality made in the correspondence with his peers and fellow embroidery lovers.[4] As Myres's widow presented them to the

Fig. 1 Robe, Rhodes, 19th century, silk on linen, 135 x 131 cm. Ashmolean Museum, EA1960.106, Bequeathed by Lady Myres, 1960

Fig. 2 Chemise, Dodecanese, 19th century, silk and metal thread on linen, 137 x 154.8 cm. Ashmolean Museum, EA1971.34, Presented by Mrs Buxton, 1971 [CAT. 19]

Ashmolean without any documentation concerning how or when they were acquired, the issue remains open.[5] Buxton's collection, finer and more varied than the former, was instead offered in memory of his wife Marjorie Buxton, a keen embroiderer herself, accompanied by his notes about their sources and purchase costs. The holdings are unlike those of Myres, who taught Buxton in Oxford, as most pieces were acquired in Britain from dealers such as Arditti & Mayorcas and Mary Bellis and private individuals between 1960 and 1970, reflecting their broader local availability at this time.[6]

As with other textile collections, the story behind the Ashmolean holdings is above all about the anonymous women who made them – and their skills. Activities such as weaving, sewing, adorning and maintaining household linens and personal clothing were, after all, among the main pursuits of women in pre-industrial societies, carried out alongside their other principal duty of childcare. Once forming the bulk of bridal trousseaux, Greek embroidered textiles were produced and cared for by women of all ages using locally produced materials: linen, cotton, silk and, to a lesser extent, wool. In traditional Aegean houses, their arrangement and display showcased the good taste and domestic talents of their makers, while also demonstrating the family's wealth and social standing, especially during festivals or special occasions **(Fig. 3)**.[7]

A mark of their creators' worth and a platform for self-expression, these textiles also helped Greek women to negotiate their place in their adult lives and associated social circles, signalling status, community membership and ethnic affiliation. Costumes displayed in museums and folk art collections, and published in recent ethnohistorical field studies, have demonstrated how coded these items could be.[8] Sometimes only minor variations were enough to convey significant social and cultural differences in certain communities.[9] Far from being merely utilitarian objects, therefore, embroideries could become effective communication tools for individuals to make statements about the place and role that they and their close relatives held within their immediate milieus.

Embroidery as an activity never disappeared from Greece, although the spread of industrialisation and manufactured goods, along with the local decline of the silk industry in the late 19th century, greatly affected this craft and the demand for fine handmade products. At this time, old embroideries turned into family heirlooms, when they were not cut up and shared between the daughters. This was particularly the case once they ceased to be a fundamental element of a bride's dowry or a regular activity during a woman's married life. As fragmentary mementos of a bygone age, these were often also the pieces bought by British collectors in the 19th and early 20th centuries. The interest and enthusiasm of these individuals eventually played a significant part in creating the collections of today's leading museums, which in many instances have become these objects' ultimate repositories.

Fig. 3 Bed arrangement for the exhibition 'Old Embroideries of the Greek Islands and Turkey' held at the Burlington Club in 1914. The textiles were lent by collectors A. J. B. Wace and R. M. Dawkins

Historic crossroads and cultural exchanges

The stylistic and technical ranges of Greek island embroideries have been traditionally explained by specialists in relation to their complex geography and historical circumstances. Byzantine, Italianate, Egyptian and Turkish influences have been pointed out in most studies of the material, with considerable attention paid to the different mechanisms of transmission (i.e. trade, migration, etc.).[10] Yet the exact dynamics of these transfers remain unclear in most instances. On the one hand, areas of the Greek archipelago belonging to the same sphere of influence show various approaches and degrees of absorption of such influxes. On the other hand, the conservative attitude of the Greek embroidery tradition, and its tendency to replicate established patterns from one generation to the next in spite of external stimuli, indicates a highly selective approach to novelties and alternative sources of inspiration. For these reasons, local circumstances and conditions can only partially account for the stylistic variations observable on surviving specimens.

The Fourth Crusade in 1204 was a turning point in the history of Greece, as it paved the way for domination by a succession of foreign powers that would last until the fight for independence (1821–32). Until then the region had been part of the Byzantine Empire, even though the formal trading privileges obtained by the Italian maritime states from Byzantium between 1020 and 1110 consolidated the presence of these powers in the trading network of the eastern Mediterranean world. Several Aegean islands benefited from this state of things and experienced significant economic growth. Their ports became vital to the expansion of trade and their products came to be in demand in Europe. These included the linen, cotton and silk at the heart of the indigenous Greek textile industry.[11]

After the sack of Constantinople in 1204, the expansion of Latin control in the region led to the creation of a series of Frankish kingdoms and duchies. Venice, which had played a crucial role in the Fourth Crusade, had the

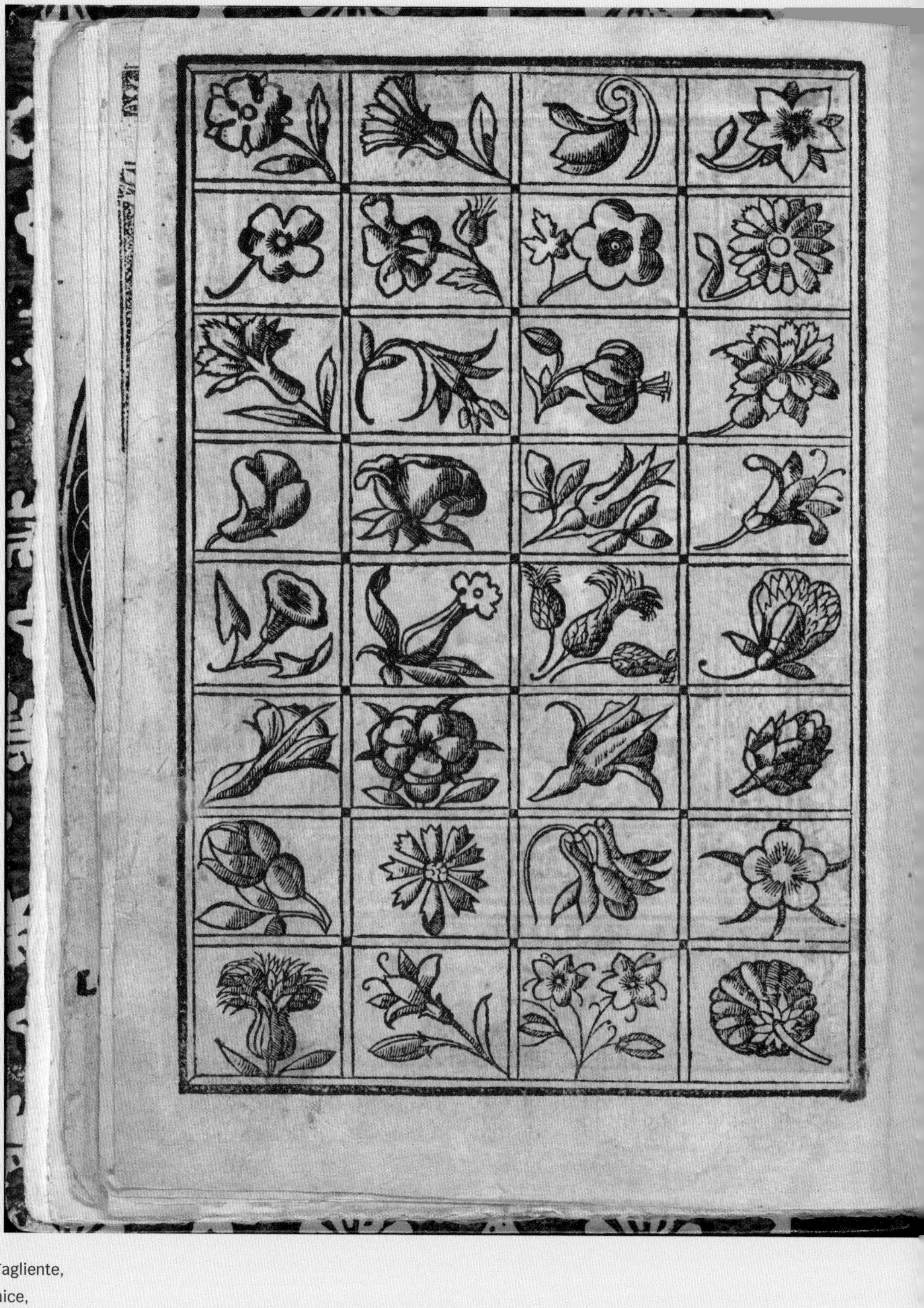

Fig. 4 Giovanni Antonio Tagliente, *Essempio di Recammi*, Venice, 1530, woodcut, page 19.8 x 15.7 cm. Metropolitan Museum of Art, 35.75.3

lion's share of the subsequent Latin carve-up of the Byzantine Empire. It bought Crete in 1204 from Boniface of Montferrat and established a duchy, the Kingdom or Duchy of Candia, which was one of only a few of its possessions to be administered directly.[12] Crete became a major commercial entrepôt in the Republic's sea empire – the Stato da màr – and a strategic bastion of its power in the east Mediterranean held until 1669, when it fell to the Ottomans.[13] Among Venice's other possessions was the Duchy of the Archipelago – or Duchy of Naxos – in the Cyclades. Here Marco Sanudo, the nephew of the Venetian doge, had established himself as ruler.[14] Consolidating what was mainly an empire of islands, in the following centuries Venice further extended its control to the Ionian islands (between the mid-14th century and the late 18th century), the island of Euboea (held until 1470) and Cyprus (conquered in 1473 but lost to the Ottomans in 1570). La Serenissima also took control of some of the coastal cities in the Peloponnese, a situation that lasted until 1540 (followed by a short-lived recapture of the region in the late 17th century).[15]

Other areas of the Aegean, such as the Dodecanese, were apportioned among other crusaders, sometimes each taking only a single island. As these knights came from different parts of Europe, the lack of any centralised control left many islands vulnerable to piracy and sporadic Turkish and Arab attacks. Some islands were also exposed to the influence of the Genoese, who were allies of the Byzantine emperors and already had a strong base in the eastern Mediterranean. This was the case for the island of Chios, for instance, which for centuries remained a cornerstone of the Genoese silk and textile industry and trade.[16] From 1250 onwards the Genoese also expanded their influence to Rhodes, the island headquarters of the Knights of the Order of St John of Jerusalem or Knights Hospitaller, until the Ottomans captured it in 1522.

The rivalry between the Latin powers and the Ottomans began shortly after the fall of Constantinople to Sultan Mehmed II (r. 1451–1481) in 1453. Between 1456 and 1458 the Turks advanced to capture the Northern Aegean, the Eastern Sporades and Athens, followed by part of the Peloponnesian peninsula. Their control of the Greek archipelago was slower to follow, however. The process began with the islands closer to the Turkish mainland, with Chios captured in 1513 and Rhodes in 1522, culminating in three Ottoman-Venetian wars which led to the Ottoman conquests of the Cyclades, the Dodecanese, Cyprus and Crete between 1537 and 1669.

These frequent changes in circumstances and the arrival of new

political and cultural interlocutors in the region have been examined closely by specialists, with a view to assessing the impact of these various foreign traditions on the local Greek textile production.[17] The influence of Venice on Greek material culture, for instance, differs from that of the Ottomans during their three centuries of rule. The islands under Venetian control were primarily ports of call for the Republic's maritime commercial activities in the eastern Mediterranean. With the exception of strategic places like Crete, therefore, local rule remained indirect and mostly entrusted to loyal members of the Venetian aristocracy and their vassals.[18] As a result, migration was the main channel for the spread of Venetian mores and culture, particularly in the urban areas.

Venetian families settled in these islands, and this often led to the hire of Greek servants in their households and Latin-Greek intermarriage. Unsurprisingly, among the incomers were embroiderers, reflecting the importance of this craft in Venetian society.[19] From the 16th century, the creative work of these expats came to be supported by pattern books, a genre of printed text that gained remarkable popularity in northern Italy and Europe at this time. Along with the above-mentioned social conditions, these books played an important part in the dissemination of foreign motifs and techniques, which were eagerly copied and adapted abroad.[20] One such text, the *Essempio di Recammi* by Giovanni Antonio Tagliente (first published in Venice in 1527), exemplifies how easy the process could be, as it includes not only an inventory of motifs for embroidery, but also instructions on how to transfer them onto cloth **(Fig. 4)**.

The Ottoman conquest did not immediately alter this situation. The Ottomans remained distanced from island life at first and, like the Venetians, they allowed a degree of local autonomy on many islands. This helped to preserve local practices and styles and to sustain established embroidery traditions. The annexation of the Aegean archipelago to the Ottoman Empire took place over an extended period of time and was achieved by different means than those of the Venetians. In particular, the forced relocation within the empire or *sürgün*, often of entire communities, was used by the Turkish sultans to consolidate their power especially in strategic areas. The process appears to have affected the smaller islands and rural communities less, limiting the resulting cultural impact.

These different policies may explain the survival of certain traditions and

Fig. 5 Detail of a bed curtain, Cyclades, 17th–18th century, silk on linen, 293 x 144 cm. Ashmolean Museum, EA1978.105.a, Presented by John Buxton, 1978 [CAT. 8]

Fig. 6 Detail of a bed curtain, Patmos, Dodecanese, 17th–18th century, silk on linen, 326.1 x 61 cm. Saint Louis Art Museum, 182: 1952, Gift of Mrs. Frank H. Cook

Fig. 7 Textile fragment with diamonds and eight-pointed stars, Egypt, 10th–15th century, silk on linen, 19 x 9.5 cm. Ashmolean Museum, EA1984.468, Presented by Professor Percy Newberry, 1941

the relatively unaltered nature of the embroideries of the more isolated islands.[21] At the same time, the increased mobility of people and objects across the whole region must ultimately have been equally responsible for the spread of embroidery designs and styles, with patterns once considered specific to certain islands adopted in other parts of the archipelago. The similarities between the embroideries of the Central and Southern Cyclades and those of Northern Dodecanese are a case in point (Figs. 5–6). They reflect types of regional exchange and interaction that stemmed from shared spheres of influence and associated local economies.[22]

Finally, international trade undoubtedly left its mark on Greek needlework. One of the most frequently cited external influences to have affected local embroideries was that of the Egyptian production in the later medieval period.[23] This came in the form of raw materials traded across the Aegean entrepôts, as well as, most likely, through finished items acquired by an increasingly wealthy local mercantile class.[24]

Textiles were an important and highly symbolic commodity in the Islamic world,[25] especially under the Mamluks (1250–1517), when changes to court ceremonials resulted in a considerable boost for this industry.[26] Therefore, in

Fig. 8 Textile fragment with stylised trees and birds, Egypt, 10th–15th century, silk on linen, 15.5 x 8.2 cm. Ashmolean Museum, EA1993.141, Presented by Professor Percy Newberry, 1941

the 13th and 14th centuries textiles accounted for some of the goods most widely traded by Egyptian merchants. Their role as 'middle-men' in the spice trade from Southeast Asia must also have provided a further stimulus for their international circulation.[27]

A number of interesting fragments in the Newberry collection of Islamic embroideries, held at the Ashmolean Museum, give us some idea of the range of weaves produced in Egypt at this time. They also provide compelling parallels for the motifs and techniques typifying the Greek embroidery tradition examined in this book.[28] The Egyptians used most of the same materials employed in the Aegean – linen for the background fabric, and silk (though in a more limited palette) for the embroidery. Egyptian examples, too, make wide use of counted thread work in cross stitch and pattern darning (Fig. 7).

These stitches played their part in the development of repeating geometric patterns and in the stylisation of naturalistic motifs such as birds and trees, establishing the basics of an imagery that was to have a broad application in later Cycladic and Dodecanese needlework (Figs. 8 & 10). A penchant for the overall repetition of shapes such as diamonds,

stars and hexagons, either in spaced arrangements or interlinked, also appears to have been shared by Mamluk and Cycladic embroiderers.

The influence of Mamluk embroideries on the Greek production remains to be fully explored. Yet Sumru Krody has recently highlighted key similarities between the two traditions in relation to the use of pattern darning, further strengthening their link. As noted in her 2006 catalogue of Greek island embroideries, 'in both cases motifs are created by the float of the running stitch on the front of the foundation fabric. The outlines and details of the motifs are formed by floating the embroidery stitch on the back.'[29] The unembroidered areas on the front become details and outlines, while a reverse image of the motif is produced, as a result, on the back. This significant technical detail confirms this as a fertile area for future research, and as one that is likely to transform what we currently know about Greek embroidery design and structure.

Fig. 9 Textile fragment with grid of lozenges, Egypt, 10th-15th century, silk on linen, 19 x 13 cm. Ashmolean Museum, EA1984.420, Presented by Professor Percy Newberry, 1941

Fig. 10 Textile fragment with stylised plants and chevron, Egypt, 10th–15th century, silk on linen, 28.5 x 14.5 cm. Ashmolean Museum, EA1993.302, Presented by Professor Percy Newberry, 1941

Greek island embroideries and Britain

The Greek island embroideries in the Ashmolean Museum in Oxford represent only one of the collections of this tradition available in Britain. In fact, in addition to the national holdings in the Victoria and Albert Museum in London, there are at least six other institutions that house significant examples of Aegean needlework.[30] Taken together, these account for the most representative gathering of this material outside of Greece.[31] Several interrelated factors led to this state of things; first, the rise of British interest in Greek archaeology and the collecting of antiquities in the late 19th and early 20th century; second, the parallel growth of anthropological and ethnographic studies; and, last, a renewed appreciation of needlework in Britain. Each of these events contributed in its own way to Greek embroidery collecting in this country, linking an interest in the aesthetic qualities of these objects to the idea that handmade textiles carry important cultural information about their makers.

During the second half of the 19th century British embroidery experienced a revival following the emergence of the Arts and Crafts Movement.[32] Born as a reaction to the negative consequences of the industrial revolution, and particularly its impact on methods of production and creativity, the Arts and Crafts advocated a return to the honesty and working principles of manual work, privileging nature, vernacular traditions and the past as sources of inspiration. A key figure in the movement and a vital contributor to the revamp of needlework was William Morris, the founder of Morris and Co., the prestigious decorative arts business responsible for commercialising individual pieces, embroidery kits and a range of other textile products (Fig. 11).

Although the work and leadership of this and other notable men, including John Ruskin, Charles R. Ashbee and Lewis F. Day, are generally openly recognised, the contributions of women to the Arts and Crafts Movement are equally noteworthy, particularly

in relation to embroidery.[33] As demonstrated by a recent exhibition, the creative achievements of Mary (May) Morris, William Morris's daughter, played a considerable part in the reassessment of this specific craft as an aesthetic as much as a practical pursuit, and in its subsequent elevation to the ranks of art.[34]

Alongside her father, May helped to popularise so-called Art Needlework, a form of embroidery based on traditional styles, free-hand drawing and vegetable-dyed silks that challenged the techniques prevalent at the time.[35] In 1875, at the young age of twenty-three, she took over the management of the embroidery department of her father's firm, training and supervising staff and providing original stylistic contributions both as a maker and as a designer **(Fig. 12)**.

This experience and her self-motivation proved essential when, after her father's death in 1896, May became responsible for the family business. But they also sustained her commitment to the emancipation of women, as her lectures and social activism attest.[36] For instance, the Women's Guild of Arts, co-founded with Mary Elizabeth Turner in 1907 and modelled on the male-only Art Workers' Guild, established a much-needed forum for female artists and designers such as Evelyn De Morgan, Mabel White and Mary Seton Watts, and an opportunity to align personal and professional development with processes of financial and political emancipation.

Progress in the education of women underpinned this and other important achievements for women's rights. In particular, the founding of the School of Art Needlework in 1872, renamed the Royal School of Needlework after receiving royal patronage in 1875, established formal training for hundreds of practitioners, professionalising the role **(Fig. 13)**. Hence, by liberating embroidery from its domestic confines and amateurish reputation, schools too played their part in enhancing this craft's artistic profile and aesthetic value, boosting its popularity across the country.

Fig. 11 William Morris (designer) and May Morris (maker), *Flowerpot*, England, 1876–1900, silk on wool, 54.6 x 54 cm. Victoria and Albert Museum, T.68-1939, Bequeathed by May Morris, 1939

Fig. 12 May Morris (designer and maker) and Theodosia Middlemore (maker), panel from the Melsetter Hangings, England, ca. 1900, wool on linen, 191.5 x 146 cm. National Museum of Scotland, K.2014.47.2, Acquired with the aid of the Art Fund and the National Museums Scotland Charitable Trust

Fig. 13 The opening of a new purpose-built centre for the Royal School of Needlework on London's Exhibition Road, 1903

The 1870s are also the time when the British began acquiring traditional costumes and embroideries in Greece. Thomas B. Sandwith was among the first to do so during his tenure as Consul of Crete between 1870 and 1885. He amassed over 160 specimens which later formed the nucleus of the Greek embroidery collection at the South Kensington Museum, London, the first of its kind to be donated to a public institution.[37]

The link between Greece, embroideries and the British progressively strengthened from this time onwards, also due, in part, to the establishment of the British School of Athens (BSA) in 1886 in support of British archaeological research in the region.[38] Following the success of the Royal School of Needlework, a parallel venture, the Royal Hellenic School of Needlework and Lace, was established in Athens in 1897 by Lady Olga Egerton, wife of the British Consul, with a view to preserving and reviving the local embroidery tradition.[39] Five years later another British woman, the embroiderer Louisa Pesel, joined the school as its director. Sharing an interest in local embroideries, she soon connected with several scholars based at the BSA who, like her, had also started acquiring local specimens.[40] Among them were the three archaeologists who later became the most prolific British collectors of Greek

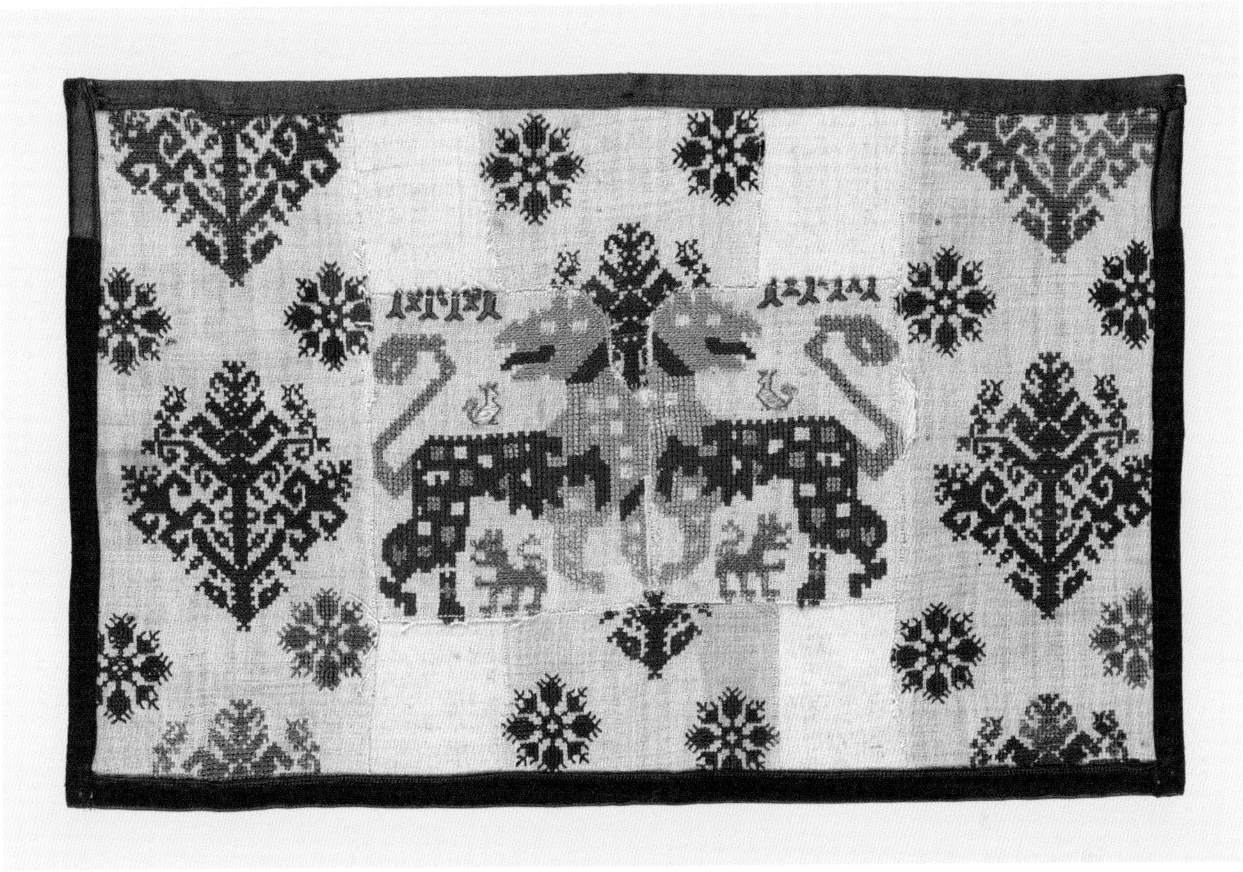

Fig. 14 Reconstituted panel with paired quadrupeds acquired by John Buxton from Souhami, a London antique textiles dealer, in 1969, Dodecanese, 18th-19th century, silk on linen, 40 x 24.5 cm. Ashmolean Museum, EA1978.119, Presented by John Buxton, 1978

needlework: Robert Carr Bosanquet, at the time director of the school; Richard MacGillivray Dawkins; and Alan John Bayard Wace.[41] Between 1919 and 1959 their legacies would go on to form the core holdings of Greek embroideries of several museums across Britain and abroad, firmly enshrining the Greek textile tradition in British institutions and the wider public imagination.[42]

Initially driven by philanthropic reasons and the desire to provide a temporary employment opportunity to refugee women escaping the Graeco-Turkish war, the Royal Hellenic School of Needlework quickly started to produce traditional Greek folk products in response to a rising foreign demand.[43] A year on from its foundation, an exhibition of the school's work took place at Liberty's famous shop on Regent Street, showcasing the work to curious and well-primed British audiences and establishing an important commercial outlet for its products.[44] Liberty's continued to supply both Greek antique and modern embroideries to British consumers for decades,[45] feeding their interest in this material after availability of authentic pieces in Greece dried up (**Fig. 14**).[46]

At the same time, along with the above-mentioned public collections, this and other popular commercial venues offered opportunities for practitioners and Arts and Crafts followers to view

foreign embroideries and draw direct inspiration from these traditions. Collectors were clearly among those who most benefited from this broadened access.[47]

Meanwhile, the cause of women's economic and political emancipation had gathered much support, including that of the Oxford collector John L. Myres **(Fig. 15)**. His studies of ancient societies delved into women's historic roles too, challenging, in particular, the idea that their subordinate position was the result of inherent weaknesses. In a well-received lecture delivered to the Liverpool Women's Suffrage Society on 8 December 1908, Myres addressed a very receptive audience, showing the value of the anthropologist's work for the 'women's question'. His views, recorded later in a newspaper article, are worth citing in full as they demonstrate his main driving principle, that of 'the past as a guide to the future':[48]

I confess that I feel as an anthropologist no surprise when I see first the fiction that women are incapable of honest work on their own independent account vanishing before the hard fact that there are thousands of women in every city who have no man to do it for them; secondly the fiction that the great mass of women are less gifted intellectually than men dispelled by the experiment of putting men and women through the same intellectual discipline; and thirdly, the fiction of the right to work, contradicted in the mouths which utter it by the claim that women have no right to work at any sort of work which can sustain a human being alive... I feel no surprise, finally, when I find that along with the growth of industries conducted by women not as members of a social group, but as individuals... there has come an unmistakable impulse to give women an equally free hand in that supreme adjustment of needful services by compromise and interchange of benefits, most responsible game of 'give and take' in which a human being can be involved at all – of which the theory is called Politics, and the Practice is Citizenship.[49]

Myres's background in classical studies provided further ground for an argument about the value of women. 'In societies which have arisen under these more varied conditions' [i.e. whose modes of subsistence were more diverse than in simple pastoral societies, such as the Greek one] his lecture continued, 'the contributions made by women's independent labour and ingenuity [are] proportionately greater.'[50] The study of these contributions and associated outputs, and their continued support in the present, were therefore deemed by Myres as something of value for society at large and not simply for those involved. In addition to revealing his progressive thinking, this

Fig. 15 Family portrait with John L. Myres and his two sons, one donning the Rhodian robe now in the Ashmolean collection, Oxford, 1912. School of Archaeology, University of Oxford, HEIR image 33956

conviction ultimately helps to explain what spurred this scholar's interest in objects produced by women's work.

The study of Greek culture, so prominent in British education at the time,[51] was undertaken by Myres during his entire career and through an impressive range of disciplinary angles.[52] His most important book, *Who Were the Greeks?*, draws on archaeological, philological, geographical, folkloric, literary and anthropological data in order to further an ethnological interpretation of the origins and progress of this people.[53] Significantly, material culture is fully integrated in his project with interesting comparisons between ancient and modern experiences.

Particularly revealing in this respect is the parallel drawn by the author between Greek modern embroidery and the geographic distribution of specific types of ancient brooches (*fibula*):

That so much concordance between material art and dialect over a period of several centuries is not fortuitous, is indicated by the striking correspondence between the geographical distribution of modern Greek dialects and the styles of embroidery, in the same region... As long as the seas are comparatively safe, standard speech and standard styles of decoration prevail; during periods of naval anarchy each district develops differently, and the boundaries of the women's art in particular are also those of the principal dialects.[54]

The suggested correspondence between objects and the linguistic features of their makers discloses, I argue, Myres's true motivation for his collecting of ethnographic evidence, including textiles. This material provided additional and reliable evidence for his research on human societies, capturing aspects of their progress. The fact that his collection does not contain objects of particular aesthetic merit or high quality might indeed ultimately reflect the way in which he thought about and used these objects. In this respect, as already noted, Myres stands apart from fellow collectors, including his own student and second Ashmolean donor John Buxton. The latter's holdings reflect a more traditional collecting approach, one that aimed for high quality, representative pieces that could be measured and evaluated against agreed standards and recognised groups of Greek island embroideries.[55]

The use of modern material culture to reconstruct patterns of human evolution was after all part of ethnological and anthropological research between the late 19th

and early 20th centuries. Objects associated with remote and non-European societies were often used to corroborate ideas on the earlier stages of European evolution, giving way to the proliferation of ethnographic collections and museums designed to sustain evolutionary theories.[56] On this matter, the work of two of Myres's contemporaries and fellow collectors, the already cited Dawkins and Wace, sheds further light on the value attributed at the time to embroideries for the study of Greek culture.[57] As noted in one of their earliest publications on the subject, the impetus to collect these textiles was not simply aesthetic but mainly driven by 'the ethnological interest of their technique and of the development of their patterns'.[58] The reasons why early collectors opted to concentrate on island needlework rather than mainland is also revealing:

The Peloponnese and the mainland Greece have never been productive of embroideries and have been overrun by invaders so often that they are Greek by culture and language rather than race… The very insularity of the other islands has modified any alien influences which have reached them, and their inhabitants, like their language and their culture, are essentially and naturally Greek. When we examine the embroideries more closely and analyze their distinctive styles we can find them a reflex of the history of the people who made them.[59]

The parallel with local dialects as quintessential sites of cultural representation, highlighted years earlier by Myres, appears again in their writings, with linguistic variations reflecting local divisions. Yet, as with other cultural products including architecture, embroideries and dialects were both deemed 'genuine products of local and native genius'.[60] Researching them, therefore, ultimately meant to capture an important facet of the Greek spirit, one of the driving objectives of early 20th-century classicists.

Even though Dawkins and Wace's achievements ended up exceeding the academic remit and entered the realm of art connoisseurship, an anthropological frame of mind underpinned their quest, one that they clearly shared with fellow classicist Myres. In Ann French's opinion, the Oxford scholar might even have been the one responsible for initiating Wace's interest, and that of others, in embroideries.[61] As Dawkins and Wace's principal acquisitions are said to coincide with their early stay in Greece (1902–14), Myres' views on Greek island needlework left a clear mark. This encounter ultimately led them to establish the foundations of a field of study that would flourish greatly in Britain and beyond in the following decades.[62]

PART II

CATALOGUE

NORTH
MACEDONIA
ALBANIA
ITALY
Ioannina
Epirus Region
Ionian
Islands

Map of modern-day Greece

From the Ionian to the Dodecanese

The embroideries in the Ashmolean Museum represent some of the traditional types associated with key areas of the Greek archipelago: the Ionian islands, the Epirus region, the Northern Sporades and Euboea, the Cyclades, the Dodecanese, and the islands of Rhodes and Crete. Below is an overview of their principal characteristics. Further information about specific uses or aspects is included in the individual catalogue entries that follow.

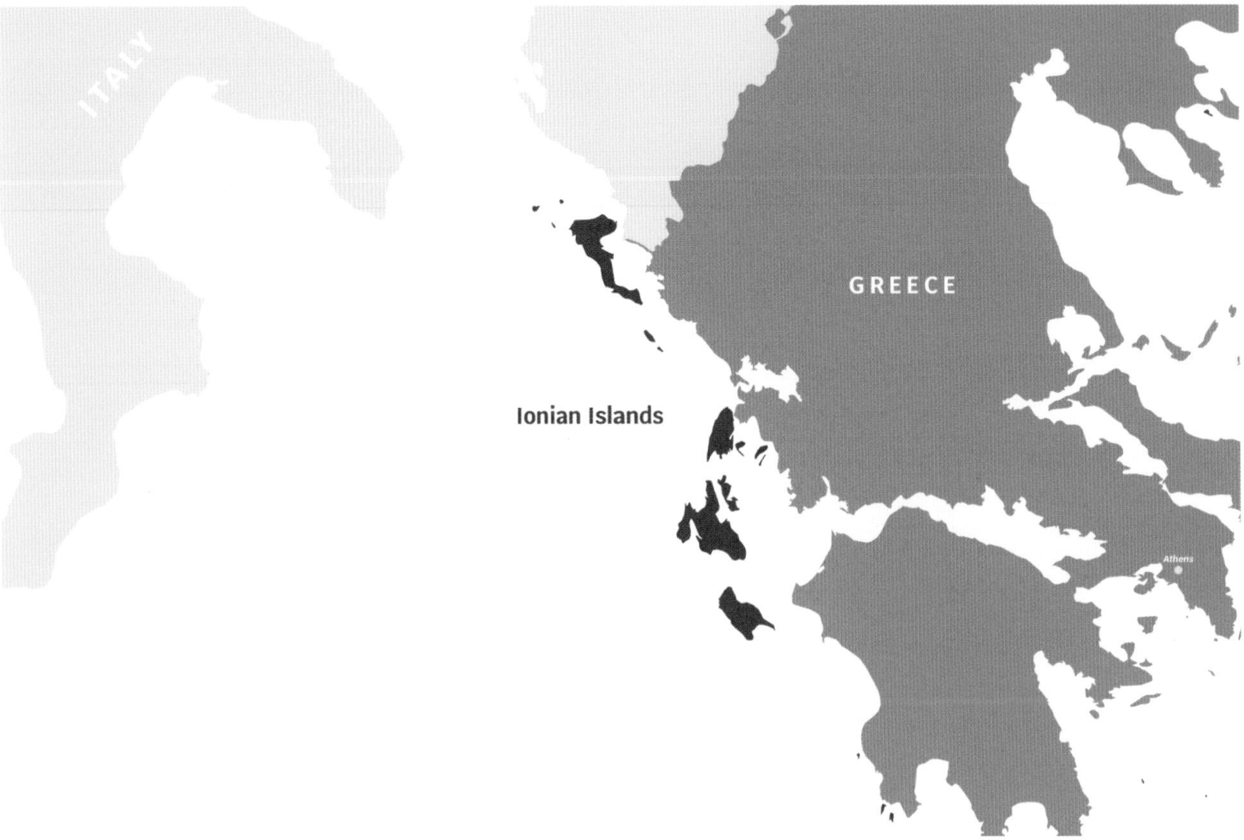

The Ionian islands

Cat. nos. 1–2

The embroideries associated with the Ionian islands are worked on an undyed linen foundation, with silk embroidery applied in a limited colour range. The primary colours, mostly red and blue, are dominant, with some yellow and medium green also used. The main decorative motifs include confronting animals (e.g. stags or other quadrupeds), peacocks, and double-headed eagles, as well as tulips and carnations. In terms of embroidery techniques, cross stitch is the most broadly attested in the region and this includes a local variant known as 'Ionian island cross stitch'.

Drawn-thread work was also widely used in the Ionian islands, but unfortunately is not represented in the Ashmolean holdings. This technique involves cutting and drawing out selected warp and weft threads from the foundation fabric to produce a netlike effect. Groups of the remaining threads are then often bound together to create a more robust grid.[1]

As both cross stitch and drawn-thread work are based on counted threads, the resulting motifs usually possess a distinctive geometric style, even when living forms are represented. For this reason, similarities with Anatolian carpets and Caucasian carpets and embroideries have been suggested, although Venetian drawn-thread work and lace, both available in this region, are more likely to have inspired this distinctive stylisation (Figs. 16-17).

Fig. 16 *Punto di Milano*, Italy, 16th–17th century, silk on linen, 13.3 x 49 cm. Museum of Fine Arts, Boston, 88.651, Benjamin Pierce Cheney Donation

Fig. 17 Cushion cover with a design similar to Anatolian carpets, Ionian islands, 18th century, silk on linen. Victoria and Albert Museum, CIRC. 840-1924

The Epirus region

Cat. nos. 3–5

Embroideries from the mainland region of Epirus have a wider range of characteristics than those from most of the Greek islands, due to the stronger impact of outside influences, especially Ottoman.[2] The most important place of production in this area was Ioannina, the Ottoman provincial capital and a thriving commercial city. Its reputation as a centre of fine embroidery is proved by the distribution of its products as far as the Balkans to the north, and Anatolia to the south.[3]

The foundation fabric in Epirus embroideries is undyed linen ranging in colour from natural to medium brown, although some of these variations could also be the effects of ageing in different environments. The designs are worked with silks in vibrant shades of red, green and blue. Brown and black are also used, but the latter has often worn away, owing to the corrosive effects of iron mordants. The motifs found on these textiles include both floral and vegetal combinations, as well as birds and groups of figures in the distinctive dress of the region. The former often reinterpret the bouquets of carnations, tulips, roses, hyacinths and serrated *saz* leaves typical of Ottoman art **(Fig. 18)**. The figural designs tend to be among the most elaborate compositions and occur on the finer embroideries, from cushions to valances and bed covers, which were made as wedding gifts **(Fig. 19)**.[4] Both types of design employ the same stitches: regular surface darning and surface darning on the diagonal, split stitch, chain stitch and herringbone stitch.

Fig. 18 Dish with tulips, carnations and serrated leaf, Iznik, Turkey, last third of the 16th century, fritware with polychrome underglaze painting, diam. 32.5 cm. Ashmolean Museum, EAX.3260, Bequeathed by J. Francis Mallet, 1947

Fig. 19 Cushion cover, Ioannina, Epirus, 17th–18th century, silk and silver thread on linen, 135 x 40.5 cm. Benaki Museum, 21173, Gift of Helen Stathatos

The Northern Sporades and Euboea

Cat. nos. 6–7

Fine, undyed, off-white linen is the typical foundation fabric for the embroideries produced in the Northern Sporades, especially Skyros and the large island of Euboea, which share several characteristics. The needlework is executed in lustrous silk, using vivid colours in vibrant juxtapositions. These complement the freely drawn motifs found scattered over the surfaces or concentrated along the borders or at the corners of each piece. Softer colours do sometimes occur but, on some pieces at least, these may just be the effects of fading.

Motifs include plump floral bouquets, sometimes in vases; human figures involved in various activities; lively birds with colourful plumage; hybrid creatures such as human-headed harpies; and ships. Some of these themes clearly reflect the strong impact of the Ottoman arts on this part of Greece, disseminated via popular goods such as textiles and ceramics (Figs. 20–21).[5] The stitches used on the embroideries from Skyros and Euboea are the most suitable for depicting these rounded, freely drawn figures. They include outline stitch, double running stitch, surface darning (both regular and on the diagonal), satin stitch and split stitch.

Fig. 20 Detail of an embroidered Ottoman cover, Turkey, 16th–17th century, silk on linen, 231 x 78.7 cm. The Textile Museum, Washington, D.C., 1.22, Acquired by George Hewitt Myers prior to 1940

Fig. 21 Plate with ship, Iznik, Turkey, 1625–1650; fritware, with polychrome underglaze painting, diam. 25.2 cm. Ashmolean Museum, EA1978.1457, Gift of Gerald Reitlinger, 1978

The Cyclades

Cat. nos. 8–18

Cycladic embroideries are possibly the most finely worked and diverse of the entire Greek archipelago, with trends and styles that can often be attributed to individual islands and centres of production. At the same time, examples from the Central and Southern Cyclades also show parallels with those of the Northern Dodecanese, both in terms of decorative motifs and in the type of articles produced, probably as a result of a degree of shared uses and customs.

Most of the surviving textiles from the Cyclades are female garments and household furnishings – above all pillowcases, bed covers, valances and curtains. The latter, generally made up of three loom-width panels, were especially popular in the region given the nature of traditional Cycladic houses. These usually consisted of a single rectangular room, with the bed at one end, hung for privacy with curtains or a tent.

The textiles associated with this region all have a neutral linen foundation and silk embroidery in bright colour combinations, mainly rose-red, a brilliant green and lemon-yellow. In some instances a single colour is dominant, as in Naxos, where embroideries make extensive use of terracotta and cardinal reds **(Fig. 22)**. However, softer tones of yellow, orange, pink and light brown also occur, especially in the production of the southern islands **(Fig. 23)**.

Fig. 22 Detail of a bedspread, Naxos, 17th–18th century, silk on linen, 120.4 x 82 cm. Ashmolean Museum, EA1978.113, Presented by John Buxton, 1978 [CAT. 11]

Cycladic embroideries feature geometric motifs such as diamonds, hexagons and stars as well as abstract designs inspired by vegetal forms. The principal foliar designs are known as the 'king' pattern or *platyphyllo* (lit. broad leaf) – with stems paired with stylised leaves at a 45-degree angle – and the 'queen' pattern or *spitha* (lit. branch) – a V-shaped form, with or without hooks, filled with stylised branches and trees sometimes flanked by birds (**Fig. 24**).[6] Both motifs also occur in other Mediterranean embroidery traditions, however. These go as far back as medieval Mamluk textiles (**Fig. 10**) or can be as recent as 19th-century Moroccan embroideries, which suggests a non-local origin.[7] Since they are based on counted-thread work, these motifs are mostly executed in running stitch (worked in different directions), as well as satin and cross stitch, including the long-armed variant.

Fig. 23 Detail of a bed valance, Cyclades, 18th century, silk on linen, 265 x 59 cm. Ashmolean Museum, EA1960.127, Bequeathed by Lady Myres, 1960 [CAT. 13]

Fig. 24 Fragment of a bed tent panel with *spitha*, Cyclades, 18th–19th centuries, silk on linen, 125.5 x 53 cm. Ashmolean Museum, EA1960.115, Bequeathed by Lady Myres, 1960

The Dodecanese islands and Rhodes

Cat. nos. 19–22

The embroideries attributed to the Dodecanese all use an undyed linen foundation. However, the fabric used on the southern islands tends to be heavier than the finer weaves of the northern islands, especially Kos and Patmos. The embroidery also differs in materials and in quality of execution, with brighter shades of pink red, pale blue, pale green and cream silk for the northern production. Thicker threads in dark green and a rich terracotta instead prevail on the more southerly islands, particularly in Rhodes, where the texture of the silk resembles the tightly curled texture of astrakhan fleece **(Fig. 25)**.[8]

Despite these differences, as mentioned earlier, much of the Dodecanese embroidery production shows close similarities with that of the Central and Southern Cyclades. Sometimes comparable designs are adopted to decorate household items that are common to both areas, especially bed tents, valances and pillowcases. In addition to the broad leaf and branch patterns noted above, the embroideries produced in the Dodecanese often use two additional repeating vegetal motifs known as *glastra* (lit. flowerpot) **(Fig. 26)**, and *dixos*, a large irregular medallion combining a leafy tree and a vase.

Although using basically similar motifs, Northern and Southern embroideries differ in terms of the thickness of the silk thread used and in the stitches. The Cycladic style is realised mainly with the finer and more versatile running stitch in pattern darning, while that of the Dodecanese is dominated instead by cross stitch in its traditional form, as well as in the plumper Rhodian variant.

Fig. 25 Detail of a bed tent panel, Rhodes, 18th–19th century, silk on linen, 201 x 80.5 cm. Ashmolean Museum, EA1960.133, Bequeathed by Lady Myres, 1960 [CAT. 22]

Fig. 26 Detail of a bed curtain with *glastra*, Dodecanese, 17th–18th century, silk on linen, 295 x 149.5 cm. Ashmolean Museum, EA1978.115, Presented by John Buxton, 1978 [CAT. 21]

Crete

Cat. nos. 23–24

Cretan embroideries stand apart from much of the Greek island production. The foundation fabric often combines linen and cotton instead of just plain linen, and the palette of the embroidery contains more colours than anywhere else. This island's production is generally subdivided into two styles: the monochrome, with embroidery executed in red or blue silk; and the polychrome, often using more than ten different hues on a single piece.

Dated examples in several collections anchor the more colourful type in the 17th and 18th centuries **(Fig. 27)**.[9] The monochrome style, instead, is thought by some to be later, owing to its less ornate appearance.[10] Yet there are also monochromatic examples that seem to be from the earlier period, leaving open the question of which came first.[11]

Despite the technical and aesthetic differences, both groups combine local patterns with adaptations of motifs of European, especially Venetian, origin. These include figures in an array of different costumes engaged in various activities (e.g. playing musical instruments, hunting, riding horses etc.). There are also mythical creatures including two-tailed mermaids, dragons, and double-headed eagles;[12] ornamental vases with flowers; and an aviary of exotic birds.

The stitches typically used on Cretan textiles include herringbone stitch, satin stitch, knot stitch, chain stitch, stem stitch and outline stitch. A type of looped stitch known as 'Cretan feather stitch' is also widely used, alongside couching and whipping, generally employed to add volume. In this respect, Cretan embroideries differ considerably from those of other Greek islands where fewer stitching techniques are usually used together on an individual piece.[13]

Fig. 27 Detail of a skirt border, signed (probably) Georgia Grammatiko, Crete, dated 1733, silk on linen, 225 x 55 cm. Victoria and Albert Museum, 2054-1876, Sandwith Collection

1

Valance border

Possibly Ionian islands, 18th century
Presented by John Buxton, 1978
Ashmolean Museum of Art and Archaeology,
University of Oxford, EA1978.118

Household furnishings, particularly bedding, account for the majority of surviving specimens of Greek island embroideries, reflecting the practical and cultural importance of these textiles in the lives of their makers. This valance border could be at home in the Ionian islands as much as in the south-eastern Cyclades. The former seems more likely, however. The colours may have faded, but a clue to this attribution could lie in the similarity to the outer border of a bedspread fragment now in The Textile Museum (**Fig. 29**).

The central section of our valance has a repeat of red confronting peacocks flanking a tulip with angular fern-like leaves. At their feet are small palmettes. The birds are drawn in some detail, with the crested heads and the 'eyes' on the tails that identify the species. The guard stripes have an in-and-out repeat of terracotta palmettes and blue leaves. The lappets along the lower edge enclose sprays of carnation and other flowers, in a format very similar to the end-borders found on Ottoman cushion covers or *yastık* (**Fig. 28**).

Foundation: warp: linen, undyed, buff colour, Z-spun, average 20 threads per cm; weft: linen, undyed, buff colour, Z-spun, average 14 threads per cm

Structure: balanced plain weave
Dimensions: 189.7 x 25.6 cm
Edge finish: one selvedge, three hemmed edges

Embroidery thread: cotton, Z2S, terracotta and blue
Embroidery stitches: cross stitch

Comments: two joined panels; lappet edging in four sections

Fig. 28 Cushion cover (*yastik*), Turkey, circa 1600, cut and voided velvet, 127 x 67.3 cm. Metropolitan Museum of Art, 17.120.123, Mr. and Mrs. Isaac D. Fletcher Collection, Bequest of Isaac D. Fletcher, 1917

Fig. 29 Bedspread fragment, Ionian islands, 18th century, silk on linen, 28 x 87 cm. The Textile Museum, Washington, D.C., 81.23, Acquired by George Hewitt Myers in 1925

2

Composite panel

Ionian islands, 18th–19th century
Bequeathed by Lady Myres, 1960
Ashmolean Museum of Art and Archaeology, University of Oxford, EA1960.125

This panel consists of three different fragments joined together. These were probably the undamaged ends from two, or possibly three, worn-out covers for bolsters, the type of long cushions used along the back of divans.[14]

The top and central sections have a repeat of tiny carnations, worked in cross stitch with red, blue and green silks, but in different directions in each instance. The middle section still has rows of stylised black leaves which are lost in the upper part. One end of each of these two sections is edged with buttonhole stitch in red and white stripes. They are now sewn together, but they were probably the end finishes of the original cover. Although embroidered in a similar palette to the top and middle segments, the lower section is more elaborate, featuring pairs of confronting birds with feathery tails that identify them as peacocks. Each of these encloses a smaller bird either in reserve or in a contrasting colour, a popular formula on the Ionian islands. The alternate registers have small green urns, or stylised cypress trees, between vases filled with single carnations and two tulips, in addition to hyacinths and tulips at the base. Framing this composition is a narrow border of oblique lozenges.

Foundation: warp: linen, undyed, buff colour, Z-spun, average 22 threads per cm; weft: linen, undyed, buff colour, Z-spun, average 16 threads per cm

Structure: balanced plain weave
Dimensions: 110 x 36.5 cm
Edge finish: two selvedges, one cut edge, one rolled and hemmed edge

Embroidery thread: silk, Z2S, light blue, dark blue, red, green, brown
Embroidery stitches: cross stitch, double running stitch, stem stitch, outline stitch, buttonhole stitch

3

Bedspread

Probably Ioannina, Epirus, 18th century
Presented by John Buxton, 1989
Ashmolean Museum of Art and Archaeology,
University of Oxford, EA1989.211

Fig. 30 Embroidered towel (*peshkir*), Turkey, 18th–19th century, silk and metal thread embroidery on cotton, 116.2. x 68.6 cm. The Cleveland Museum of Art, 1916.1249, Gift of Mr and Mrs J. H. Wade

Like numerous Greek bedspreads, particularly from Epirus, this example appears to have been reconstituted from a damaged piece by adding a new, plain central panel to the original borders.[15] These are richly embroidered with a repeat of a red flower clasped by two flowering green stems. The areas around this motif are filled with a dense yet orderly arrangement of smaller stylised blooms and leaves in several colours. Some details are in white, while most of the design elements were once outlined in black, now almost entirely lost owing to corrosion. The narrower borders framing these central friezes feature deeply indented off-white bands punctuated by tiny green and red buds.

The formula of continuous vegetal scrolls inscribing single vegetal and floral motifs was especially popular in the Ottoman textile tradition, with impressive combinations on luxury fabrics such as brocades and velvets (**Fig. 31**). The flower between serrated leaves featured on this bedspread only distantly echoes these fine designs, but it evokes contemporaneous Turkish embroideries which must have circulated more easily in the area of Greece when the original coverlet was made (**Figs. 30 & 32**).

Foundation: main field warp: linen, undyed, pale yellow, Z-spun, average 20 threads per cm; main field weft: linen, undyed, pale yellow, Z-spun, average 19 threads per cm; border warp: linen, undyed, off-white, Z-spun, average 22 threads per cm; border weft: linen, undyed, off-white, Z-spun, average 24 threads per cm

Structure: balanced plain weave
Dimensions: 218 x 182 cm
Edge finish: two selvedges, two hemmed edges concealed by lining

Embroidery thread: silk, Z2S, cream, beige, lime green, olive green, khaki green, pale pink, amaranth red, apricot orange, light blue, black
Embroidery stitches: herringbone stitch, outline stitch, split stitch

Comments: traces of the design drawn on the front of the fabric before embroidery

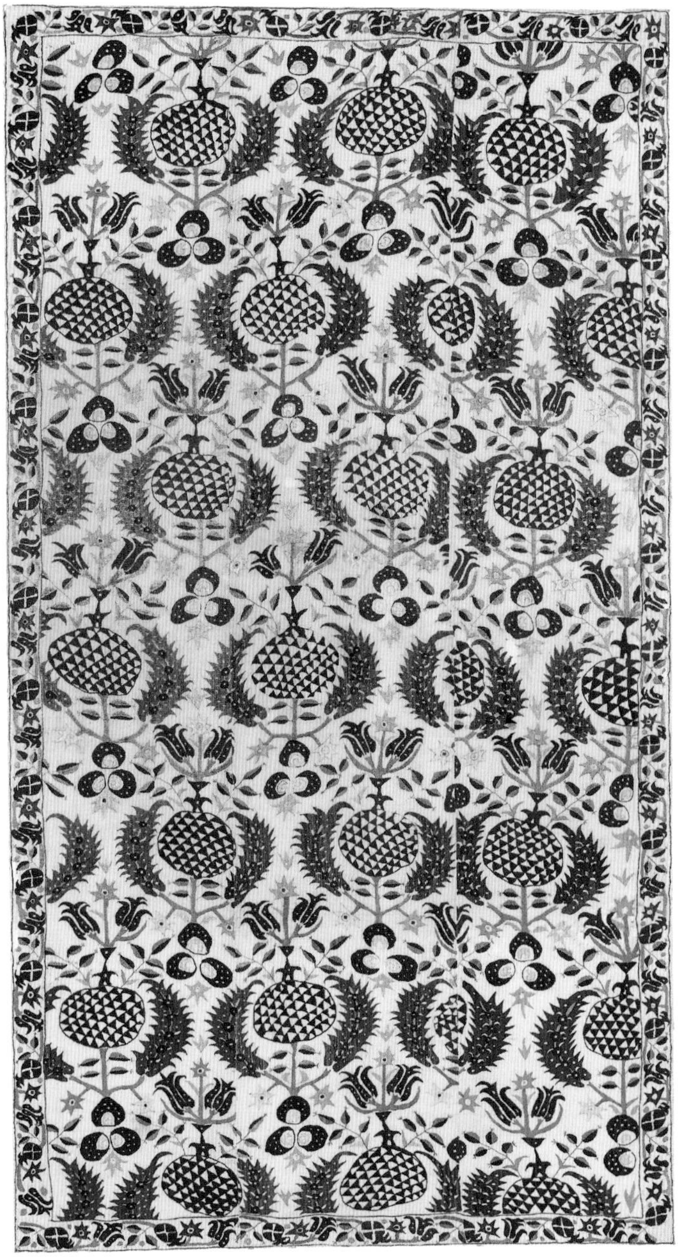

Fig. 31 Ottoman velvet with pine cones and paired *saz* leaves, probably Bursa, Turkey, early 17th century, silk and metal-wrapped thread, 157.5 x 63 cm. Kunstgewerbemuseum, Staatliche Museen zu Berlin, 1884.903

Fig. 32 Ottoman embroidery with pomegranates and paired *saz* leaves, probably Epirus, silk on linen, late 16th–17th century, 237 x 130 cm. Ashmolean Museum, EA2007.104, Purchased with the assistance of the MLA/V&A Purchase Grant Fund, 2007

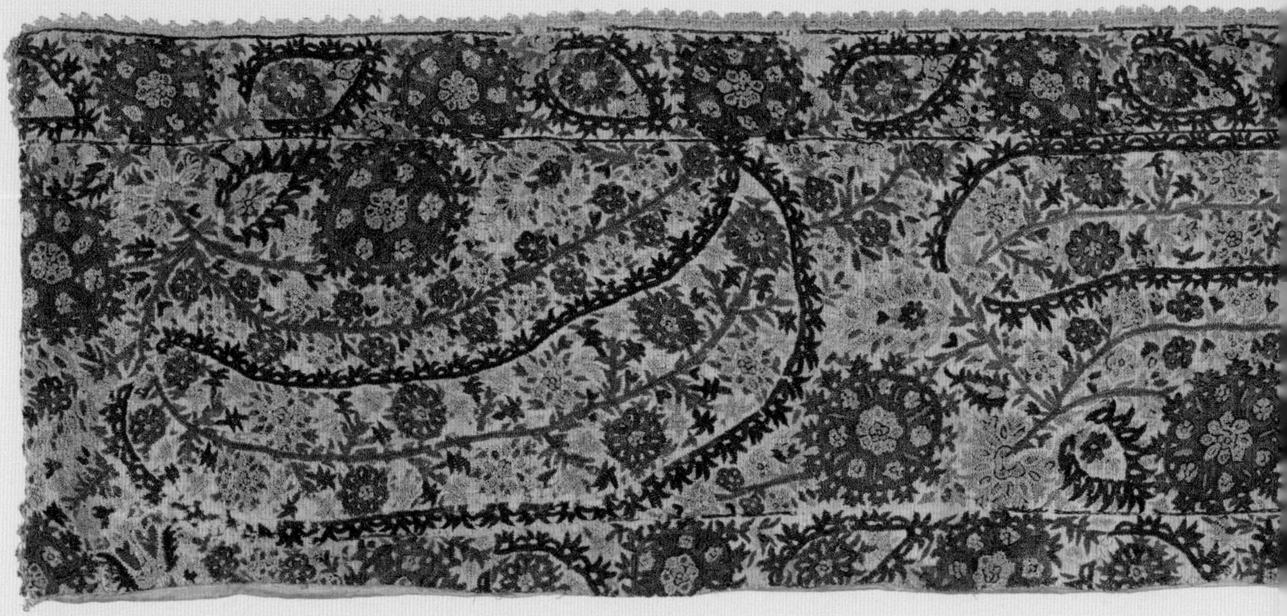

4

Border fragment of a bedspread or cover

Probably Ioannina, Epirus, 18th–19th century
Presented by John Buxton, 1978
Ashmolean Museum of Art and Archaeology,
University of Oxford, EA1978.104

Fig. 33 Cover made of three joined borders, Ioannina, Epirus, 18th–19th century, silk on linen, 186 x 135 cm. The Textile Museum, Washington, D.C., 1962.23.3, Museum Purchase

This border fragment carries an intricate design, one that is found on a distinctive group of 18th- to 19th-century Epirote embroideries associated with Ioannina. The central field has three repeats of the main pattern unit, facing in alternate directions. Each unit comprises a spray of three flowering stems growing from a single branch, but dominated by a large, sickle-shaped leaf reminiscent of the Ottoman *saz* leaf.[16] With a lace-like edging of dark blue stylised trefoils, this leaf encloses another stem with smaller red flowers. The remaining background is then filled with serrated palmettes and elaborate red floral rosettes, a combination that is also repeated, in tighter sequence, along the narrow outer borders.

Borders of this type were made for bedspreads or valances, but have rarely survived in their original form.[17] They were often re-joined, combining two or three widths, to become new functional covers (**Fig. 33**). Valances and covers of this type were generally used in Epirote living areas to cover low divans alongside matching cushions.[18]

Foundation: warp: linen, undyed, buff colour, Z-spun, average 24 yarns per cm; weft: linen, undyed, buff colour, Z-spun, average 25 threads per cm

Structure: balanced plain weave
Dimensions: 154 x 32.5 cm
Edge finish: one selvedge, three hemmed edges under a silk lining

Embroidery thread: silk, Z2S and Z3S, beige, carmine red, brown, powder blue, light blue, dark blue
Embroidery stitches: herringbone stitch, chain stitch, outline stitch

Comments: two linings, an older and possibly original one in linen, and a second in pink silk; one edge trimmed with crochet, possibly added at the same time as the silk lining; traces of the underdrawing onto the front before embroidery

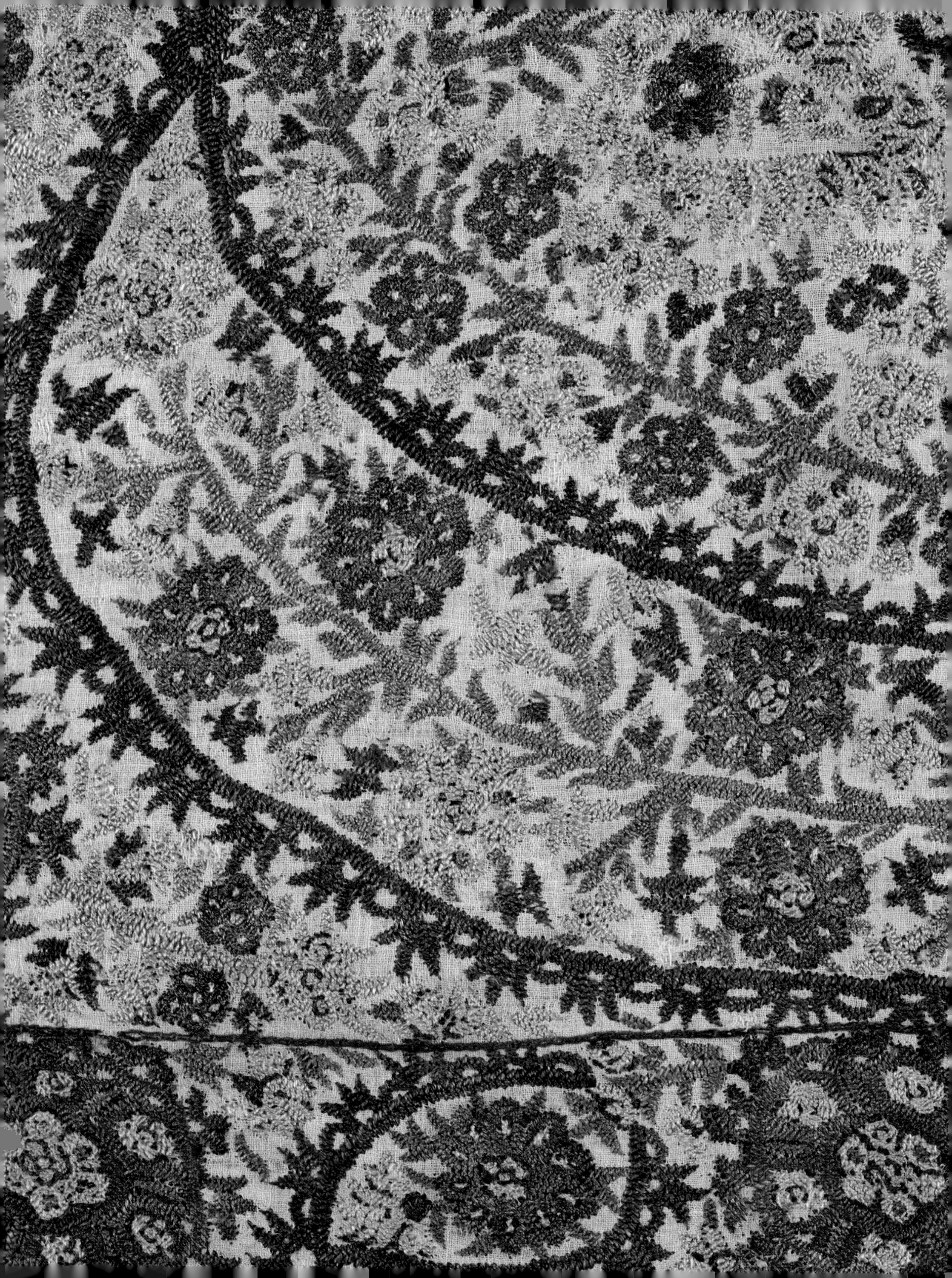

5

Border fragment of a bedspread or sheet

Probably Epirus, 18th–19th century
Bequeathed by Lady Myres, 1960
Ashmolean Museum of Art and Archaeology,
University of Oxford, EA1960.140

Of all the Greek embroideries in the Ashmolean collection, this lively border is among the ones with the strongest affinity to classical Ottoman ornament. Its continuous scroll of coiling, serrated leaves and small red buds echoes the blooming trellises of *saz* leaves so typical of Ottoman art and found on a range of objects **(Fig. 34)**. On our fragment, further movement is created by additional scrolling, leafy ribbons in red and green silk. These encircle a smaller serrated leaf and red flower to create irregular medallions. As with the other decorative borders seen so far in this catalogue, the central section is framed by two narrower bands, here decorated with a repeat of stylised trefoils in alternating colours. A woven braid was probably added at a later time to finish the border.

There are no immediate parallels among published examples. Two other sections, probably originating from the same original piece, exist in the Ashmolean collection. Judging by their dimensions, this must once have been a large textile, a bedspread or sheet.[19]

An attribution to either Epirus or Skyros could be suggested for the group. However, both the colours and the looser manner of working the surface darning on the diagonal point at Epirus as their most likely place of production. The trefoil border is sometimes seen on Ottoman embroideries, some of which are also believed to have been made in Epirus for the Ottoman market.

Foundation: warp: linen, undyed, off-white, Z-spun, average 21 yarns per cm; weft: linen, undyed, off-white, Z-spun, average 18 threads per cm

Structure: balanced plain weave
Dimensions: 64.2 x 14.2 cm
Edge finish: three hemmed edges, one cut edge

Embroidery thread: silk, Z2S, cream, red, green, blue
Embroidery stitches: surface darning on the diagonal

Comments: remains of a joining stitch along the top edge

Fig. 34 Tile with *saz* leaves and flowers, Turkey, second half of the 16th century, fritware with polychrome underglaze painting, 26.1 x 26.1 cm. Ashmolean Museum, EAX.3215

6

Fragment of a cover with cockerel

Skyros, Northern Sporades, 18th century
Bequeathed by Lady Myres, 1960
Ashmolean Museum of Art and Archaeology,
University of Oxford, EA1960.153

Fig. 35 Part of bedspread, Skyros, Northern Sporades, 18th century, silk on linen, 219 x 83 cm. The Textile Museum, Washington, D.C., 81.80, Acquired by George Hewitt Myers in 1927

Despite having lost its legs, the cockerel on this fragment still retains the liveliness that is so typical of the embroideries from Skyros. The island is thought to have been the only one in the Northern Sporades to have produced a distinctive embroidery style during the period considered by this book.[20] The use of bold colour juxtapositions in the cusped stripes is a hallmark of its production, which adapted the Ottoman way of handling blocks of solid colour on embroidery (**Fig. 36**).

A number of examples with similar cockerels can be found in various collections (**Fig. 35**). The more complete pieces also give us some idea of the possible original context of our fragment. Traces of plaited insertion stitch along its top border suggest that this too was once part of a wider section, possibly attached to one or more loom-widths to form a cover of sorts. Fabric with this design could also be utilised for smaller items such as cushion covers.

Foundation: warp: linen, undyed, off-white, Z-spun, average 21 threads per cm; weft: linen, undyed, off-white, Z-spun, average 21 threads per cm

Structure: balanced plain weave
Dimensions: 54.2 x 32 cm
Edge finish: one selvedge, three cut edges

Embroidery thread: silk, Z3S, white, light pink, dark pink, lemon-yellow, light blue, teal, brown, some corroded black
Embroidery stitches: surface darning on the diagonal, double running stitch, outline stitch, plaited insertion stitch

Fig. 36 Detail of a panel with floral decoration, Turkey, 19th century, silk on cotton, 106 x 46 cm. Private collection

7

Bedspread

Skyros, Northern Sporades, 18th–19th century
Presented by John Buxton, 1978
Ashmolean Museum of Art and Archaeology,
University of Oxford, EA1978.116

The deep border of this bedspread has a repeat of floral bouquets in small vases, all facing inwards towards a plain centre. Each ensemble has two lateral branches and a central stem with a heart-shaped floret and, above it, sprays of stylised flowers and leaves flanked by small cockerels. The colours are unusually quiet for a Skyros embroidery, but this may be the effect of extended use and fading. The light texture of the linen ground may be a further sign of this piece's fragile condition.

The coverlet is made up of eight panels that probably come from a larger, damaged piece refurbished at some point. The tassels are also a likely later addition, possibly dating from the same period as the cypress trees, which appear to be the work of a less skilled hand than the author of the original design.

Foundation: warp: linen, undyed, off-white, Z-spun, average 20 threads per cm; weft: linen, undyed, off-white, Z-spun, average 22 threads per cm

Structure: balanced plain weave
Dimensions: 220 x 122 cm
Edge finish: four hemmed edges

Embroidery thread: silk, Z2S and single untwisted thread, cream, beige, light pink, dark pink, powder-blue, light blue, brown
Embroidery stitches: surface darning worked in different directions, outline stitch, satin stitch, whip stitch

Comments: some edges joined with whip stitch, and some with French seams; some areas show later darning stitches

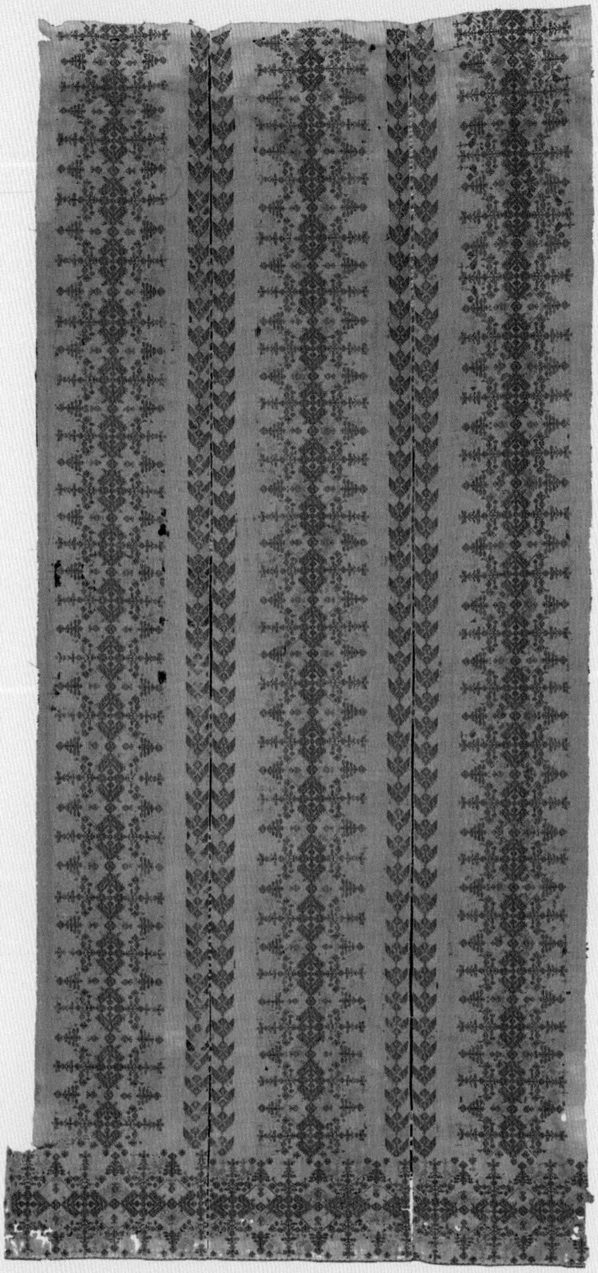

8

Bed curtain

Cyclades, 17th–18th century
Presented by John Buxton, 1978
Ashmolean Museum of Art and Archaeology,
University of Oxford, EA1978.105a

This nearly complete bed curtain testifies to the extraordinary finesse of the embroideries produced in the central and southern Cyclades. These panels were used in Cycladic interiors to separate the sleeping quarters from the rest of the house, which often consisted of a single rectangular room (Fig. 37). As the entrance was usually in the opposite short side of this space, hangings like this provided an attractive focal point while flaunting the family's taste and wealth.

Three intricately worked columns dominate this piece, with the same design along the lower edge, but worked horizontally as a border. The central section is the only complete loom-width and retains the embroidered side borders missing from the outer edge of the lateral sections. Plaited insertion stitches were used to attach the three main panels to each other.

The decoration is a sum of the motifs typical of the region.[21] The central spine is made from a series of medallions obtained by facing pairs of V-shaped motifs. These are further linked by a succession of small lozenges, some with swastikas. Either side of these there were once pairs of peacocks, in blue-green and black, now lost owing to corrosion. Other black details have also disappeared, with only a few traces left. Trees grow horizontally to right and left of the columns, with a double-headed eagle flanked by green confronting peacocks at the tip of every alternate tree. On either side of this central motif are ascending borders of paired leaves in a geometric variant of the *platyphyllo* or 'king' pattern.[22] These are tightly packed but still show traces of the darker brown threads used in some places. Small squares in the leaves enclose tiny quadrupeds, each with a lifted front paw, a possible reference to the lion of St Mark, the patron saint of Venice.[23]

The charm of this type of embroidery is in the detail, much of it in reserve. Each of the larger pattern units is a warren of smaller elements which, combined, create a look unique to the textiles associated with this area of the Aegean.

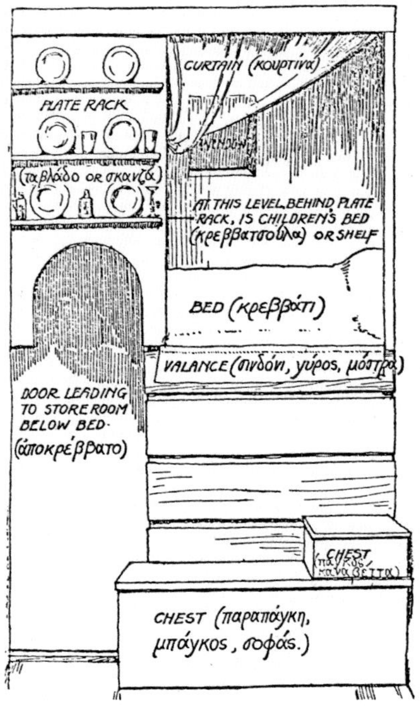

. Ὄψη ὑπερυψωμένου χώρου γιά ὕπνο στίς Κυκλάδες (πηγή: Dawkins-Wace. "The towns and houses of the Archipelago", 105).

Fig. 37 Sketch-elevation of Cycladic bed-platform, after A. J. B. Wace and R. M. Dawkins, 'Greek Embroideries – II: The Towns and Houses of the Archipelago', *The Burlington Magazine for Connoisseurs*, 26, 141 (Dec. 1914), p.105, fig. 4

Foundation: warp: linen, undyed, medium brown, Z-spun, average 18 threads per cm; weft: linen, undyed, medium brown, Z-spun, average 19 threads per cm

Structure: balanced plain weave
Dimensions: 293 x 144 cm
Edge finish: one selvedge, one cut edge, one edge cut and hemmed in buttonhole stitch, one hemmed edge

Embroidery thread: silk, S2Z, cream, brick red, green, brown, black
Embroidery stitches: surface darning on the diagonal, running stitch, satin stitch, insertion stitch, buttonhole stitch

9

Cushion cover

Naxos, Cyclades, 17th–18th century
Presented by John Buxton, 1978
Ashmolean Museum of Art and Archaeology,
University of Oxford, EA1978.106

This pillow face introduces a style that has been securely associated by specialists with the island of Naxos, at the heart of the Cyclades. The island was the seat of the Duchy of Naxos, established by Venice in the immediate aftermath of the Fourth Crusade (1204), with power stretching over the rest of the Cyclades and part of the Northern Dodecanese. It thus gained considerable economic prosperity, which is reflected in its distinctive and rich embroidery tradition.[24]

Like other examples from this island, this cushion cover has a well-balanced design in which the reserved areas between the coloured zones are cleverly juxtaposed to create the pattern. The embroidery, in red silk, is worked in two directions, in order to capture the tonal variations of this material as each area catches the light differently. This technique, using in fact only one shade of red silk, is a well-known feature of Naxos embroideries, although green and blue occasionally enrich its palette in some examples.

The design is very subtle on this piece, and among the most accomplished of the Ashmolean embroideries associated with Naxos. At first glance it consists of a diagonal lattice formed by large diamonds that enclose indented cruciform motifs surrounded by angular hooks. However, these crosses face in different directions in alternate rows, so that the horizontal and vertical lines running through the centre of each create a secondary square grid. The careful siting of the small blue and green 'X's highlights the corners of each square. At the crossing of the diagonals within each square, small triangles face outwards. These draw the eye to two concentric octagons formed by lines with hooks at each end facing inwards.

This cushion cover also demonstrates the repurposing that many Greek embroideries underwent over time, as it was probably once part of a much larger textile. It still has some of the original border, with a repeat of diamonds and S-shaped motifs. This is similar to the border of an Egyptian embroidery in the Ashmolean (**Fig. 38**), a detail that further supports the idea of Egypt's influence on Greek island designs.[25]

Foundation: warp: linen, undyed, buff colour, Z-spun, average 22 threads per cm; weft: linen, undyed, buff colour, Z-spun, average 21 threads per cm

Structure: balanced plain weave
Dimensions: 40 x 31.3 cm
Edge finish: one selvedge, three cut edges

Embroidery thread: silk, S2Z, red, green and blue
Embroidery stitches: surface darning worked in different directions

Comments: one side appears hand-sewn while the remaining three appear machine stitched; later cotton backing

10

Section of a bedspread

Naxos, Cyclades, 17th–18th century
Presented by John Buxton, 1978
Ashmolean Museum of Art and Archaeology,
University of Oxford, EA1978.114

Probably about half of a complete bedspread, this large cover is another example of the ingenuity of Naxos embroidery designers. It is made up of two complete loom-widths whose end warps are twisted into fringes.

As with Cat. 9, the ground is covered with a lattice of large diamonds, each enclosing a hooked and toothed cruciform motif. At the centre of each cross is an eight-pointed star, with four tiny triangles in the middle that turn like a windmill. Yet the secondary pattern is harder to spot than in the previous piece, as the horizontal and vertical lines are less well defined, and small differences in the minor details deflect the eye. There is also a narrow border along both ends and down one side with a repeat of hexagonal lozenges in reserve enclosing S shapes.

As on most Naxos embroidery, the ground is covered with red silk embroidery, which is worked in different directions, so that the colours change in intensity as the piece is moved about. It is interesting to compare this piece with Cat. 12, which lacks the two-tone effect as a result of the single direction followed by the stitches.

Foundation: warp: linen, undyed, buff colour, Z-spun, average 17 threads per cm; weft: linen, undyed, buff colour, Z-spun, average 17 threads per cm

Structure: balanced plain weave
Dimensions: 225 x 96 cm
Edge finish: two selvedges, two edges with warp-ends twisted into fringes

Embroidery thread: silk, Z-spun and Z2S, red
Embroidery stitches: surface darning worked in different directions

Comments: repaired with matching patches, probably from the missing section

11

Section of a bedspread

Naxos, Cyclades, 18th century
Presented by John Buxton, 1978
Ashmolean Museum of Art and Archaeology,
University of Oxford, EA1978.113

Fig. 38 Textile fragment with diamonds and geometric patterns, Egypt, 13th–15th century, cotton embroidery on linen, 57 x 35.8 cm. Ashmolean Museum, EA1993.75, Presented by Professor Percy Newberry, 1941

A section of a much larger textile but retaining two of the original outer borders, this bedspread showcases an inventive use of a popular Cycladic decorative motif: the *platyphyllo*.[26] Its single leaf unit is here used as the building block of an X-shaped pattern which has been embroidered in continuous, parallel rows over the entire surface of the fabric.[27] The interstitial spaces are filled with octagonal motifs obtained by two intersecting crosses and four arrowhead protrusions. The border of this embroidery has a repeat of small lozenges in reserve, resembling a twisted ribbon.

The changing colour densities of the areas worked at a different angle mean that the decorative motifs can be read in other ways: a grid of diamonds linked by small cubes, the diamonds in one horizontal row darker than the next; a repeat of circles, with their outlines created by the unembroidered areas; or a square trellis enclosing foliar saltires, with eight-pointed stars in reserve at the crossing points.

In 1983 James Trilling provocatively argued for the influence of lacework design and pattern books on Naxos embroideries (Fig. 39).[28] The more spaced distribution of the individual geometric motifs on this bedspread, unlike the dense pattern darning more typical of the examples as illustrated in Cats. 9, 11 and 12, could make a good case for such cross-pollination among sister crafts. At the same time, a taste for repeating geometric forms also characterised the Egyptian embroidery production under the Mamluks. Considering the geographical proximity and the longevity of the Egyptian textile trade in the eastern Mediterranean, Mamluk embroideries represent an equally viable, if not more likely, source of inspiration for these distinctive textiles, one that is also closer in technical terms (Fig. 38).

Foundation: warp: linen, undyed, off-white, Z-spun, average 15 threads per cm; weft: linen, undyed, off-white, Z-spun, average 15 threads per cm

Structure: balanced plain weave
Dimensions: 120.4 x 82 cm
Edge finish: one selvedge, two cut edges, one edge with warps twisted into a fringe

Embroidery thread: silk, Z2S, red
Embroidery stitches: surface darning worked in different directions

Fig. 39 Page from Jacques Foillet, *Nouveaux pourtraicts de point coupé*, Montbeliard, 1598. Bibliothèque nationale de France, département Estampes et photographie, RESERVE 4-LH-105

12

Bedspread or curtain

Naxos, Cyclades, 18th century
Presented by John Buxton, 1978
Ashmolean Museum of Art and Archaeology,
University of Oxford, EA1978.201

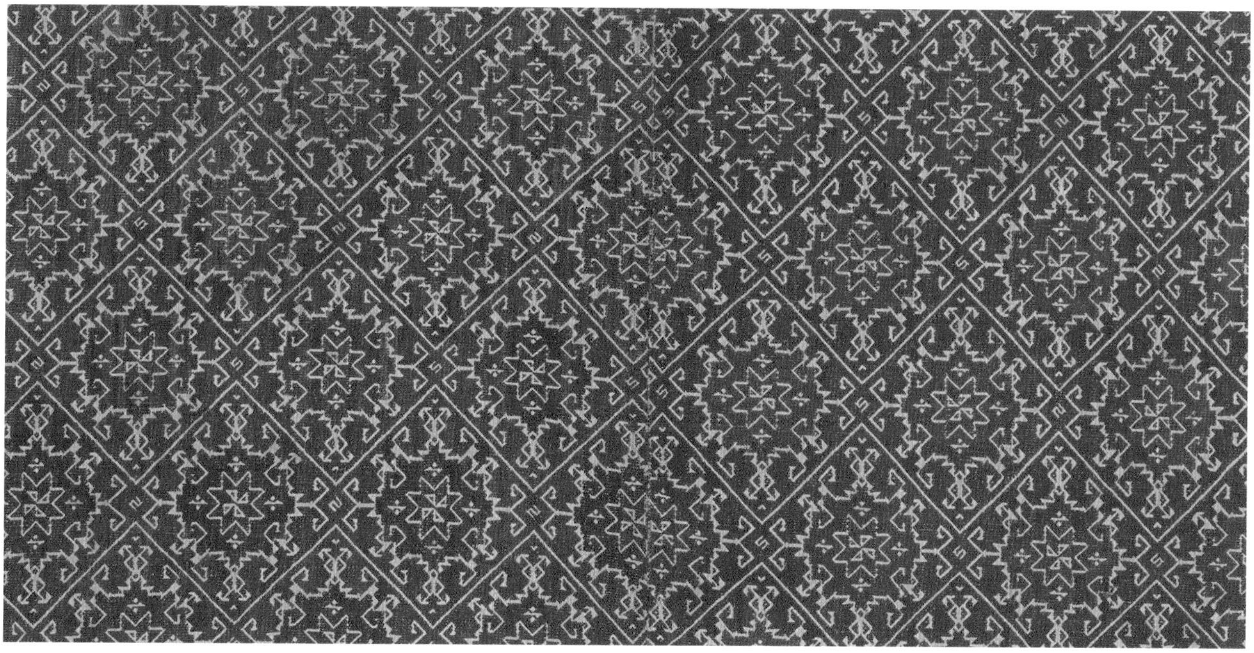

An almost complete example, this cover consists of three loom-width panels plus a fourth cut section. The overall effect of its design is almost baroque, like an opulent brocaded silk fabric. Unlike that of Cats. 9, 10 and 11, the embroidery is worked in only one direction, resulting in a more uniform colour and overall texture. Yet one can still discern the different patterns at work, including several geometric combinations.

The reserve pattern produces curved vertical brackets that the eye can manipulate into a variety of shaped medallions with cusped outlines. These are overlaid with a geometric trellis of large interlinked diamonds, each enclosing a central star. Though less disciplined, this motif of a star with a jagged surround is not unlike those on Cats. 9 and 10.

Foundation: warp: linen, undyed, buff colour, Z-spun, average 17 threads per cm; weft: linen, undyed, buff colour, Z-spun, average 17 threads per cm

Structure: balanced plain weave
Dimensions: 231.2 x 186 cm
Edge finish: one cut edge, one selvedge turned under, two edges hemmed

Embroidery thread: silk, S2Z, red
Embroidery stitches: surface darning, worked in the same direction

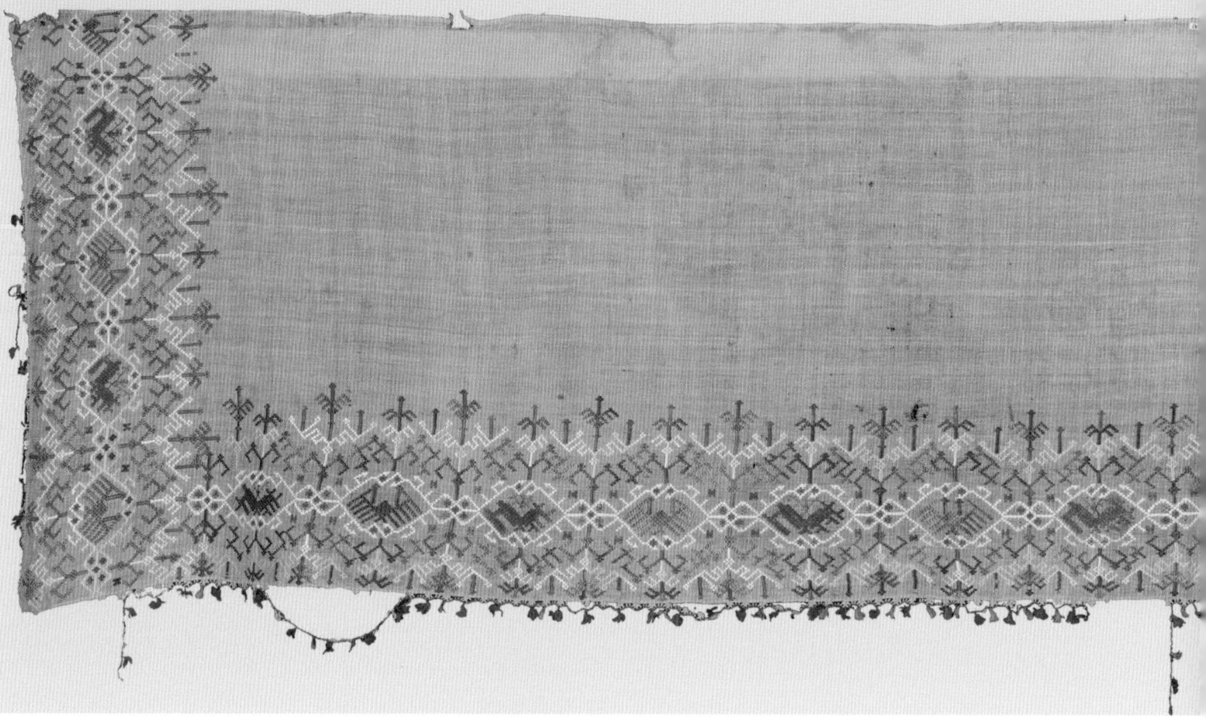

13

Bed valance

Cyclades, 18th century
Bequeathed by Lady Myres, 1960
Ashmolean Museum of Art and Archaeology,
University of Oxford, EA1960.127

The embroidery on this piece is worked on both the front and back of a lightweight linen, so the design is reversible. Double-sided embroidery was usually employed when both sides of the piece would be seen during use, so mostly for valances, towels and sashes. In the case of valances, these were often made in pairs, with the two sections shown together, one above the other and the sides folded inwards, to reveal more of the decorated area (**Fig. 3**).

Although executed in delicate pastel shades, and much simplified, the design is based on the same formula as the more brightly coloured border on Cat. 8. Such fine linen would not be strong enough to support the weight of the extra silk needed for a more complex version of the design. The cost of the silk may also have been a factor, or just personal preference.

As on many other Cycladic embroideries, the stitches are worked in different directions so that the change in the depth of colour adds to the overall decorative effect. For example, the main element of the repeat, the white central horizontal chain of hooked cartouches, is worked vertically.

Only a few coloured minor details lie in the same direction, while the stitches of the leaves and tree branches, forming a zig-zag frieze along the outer border, are on the horizontal and therefore appear slightly darker. The rest of the design is also worked on the horizontal, including the double-headed eagles inhabiting the central chain of lozenges. This sequence is reversed on the vertical side borders, but the result is the same. The strategic use of white and cream silk draws the eye towards the relevant pattern elements, so that the overall effect is more like lace rather than the heavily embroidered variants of this formula seen elsewhere in this region.[29]

Foundation: warp: linen, undyed, off-white, Z-spun, average 15 threads per cm; weft: linen, undyed, off-white, Z-spun, average 13 threads per cm

Structure: balanced plain weave
Dimensions: 265 x 59 cm
Edge finish: two selvedges, two hemmed edges

Embroidery thread: silk, single and double untwisted thread, cream, burnt-orange, green, light blue
Embroidery stitches: satin stitch

Comments: edged with needle-lace, with tassels in green and a pale salmon-pink

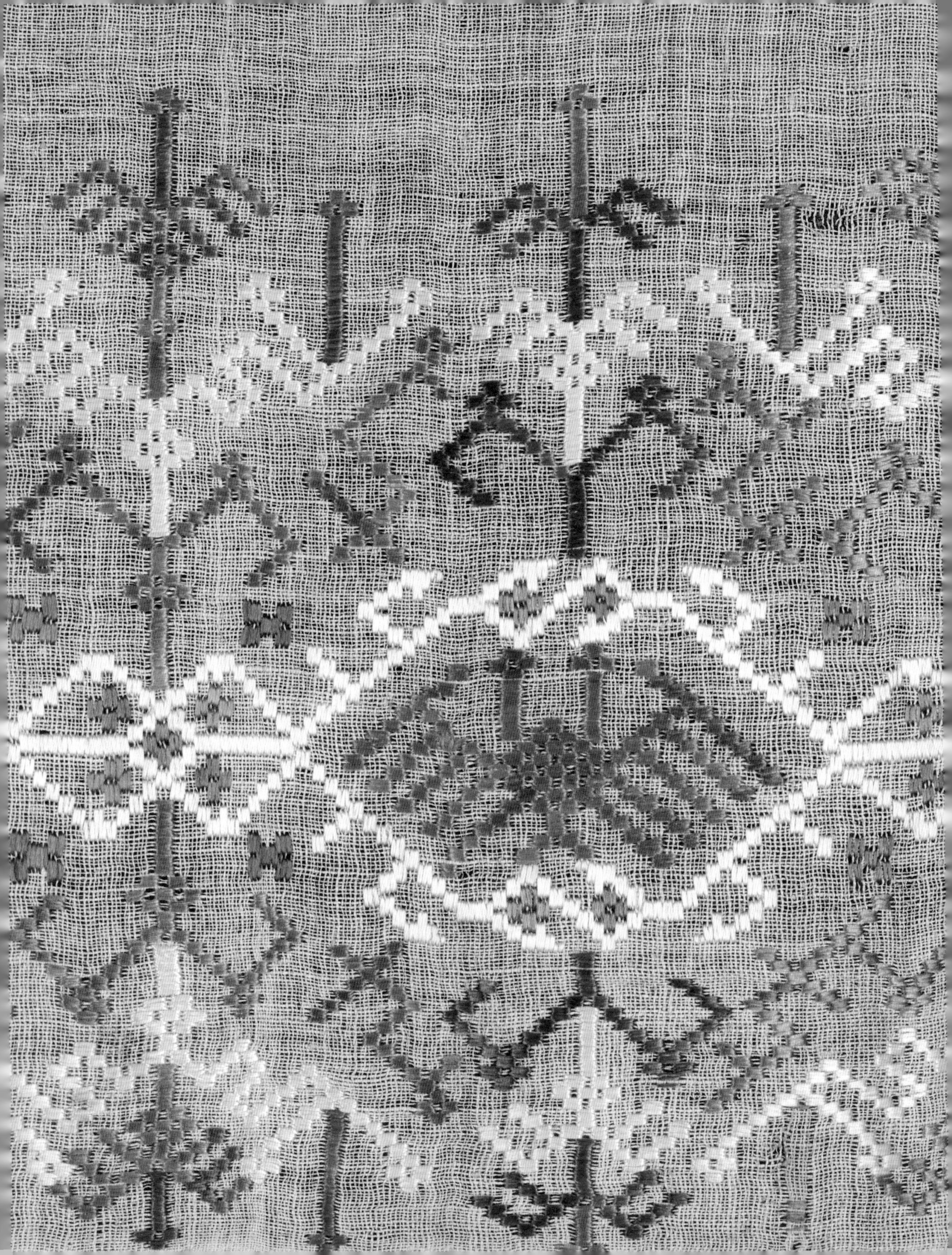

14

Cushion cover

Possibly Anafi, Cyclades, 18th century
Bequeathed by Lady Myres, 1960
Ashmolean Museum of Art and Archaeology,
University of Oxford, EA1960.113

A regular item in Greek island homes, cushion covers were just as much decorated with embroidery as their larger siblings. Cushions were piled up in a neat stack by the bed, so only the front and sides would be visible (**Fig. 3**). As on the example illustrated here, often only three sides were decorated, as the fourth would face the back and thus remain hidden.[30]

In Cycladic covers, the design is generally executed in cross stitch, including the long-armed variant, which calls for geometric designs. In this instance, quartered squares within eight-pointed stars alternate with a motif with a central lozenge linked by a stem to the blue paired leaves at each end. The borders are framed within dark-cream guard stripes, worked in long-arm cross stitch with a simple repeat of voided squares.

Foundation: warp: linen, undyed, off-white, Z-spun, average 15 threads per cm; weft: linen, undyed, off-white, Z-spun, average 13 threads per cm

Structure: balanced plain weave
Dimensions: 49.5 x 42 cm
Edge finish: three seams with selvedges, one open edge

Embroidery thread: silk, Z2S, in beige, yellow, light blue, dark blue, light green and red
Embroidery stitches: cross stitch, long-armed cross stitch

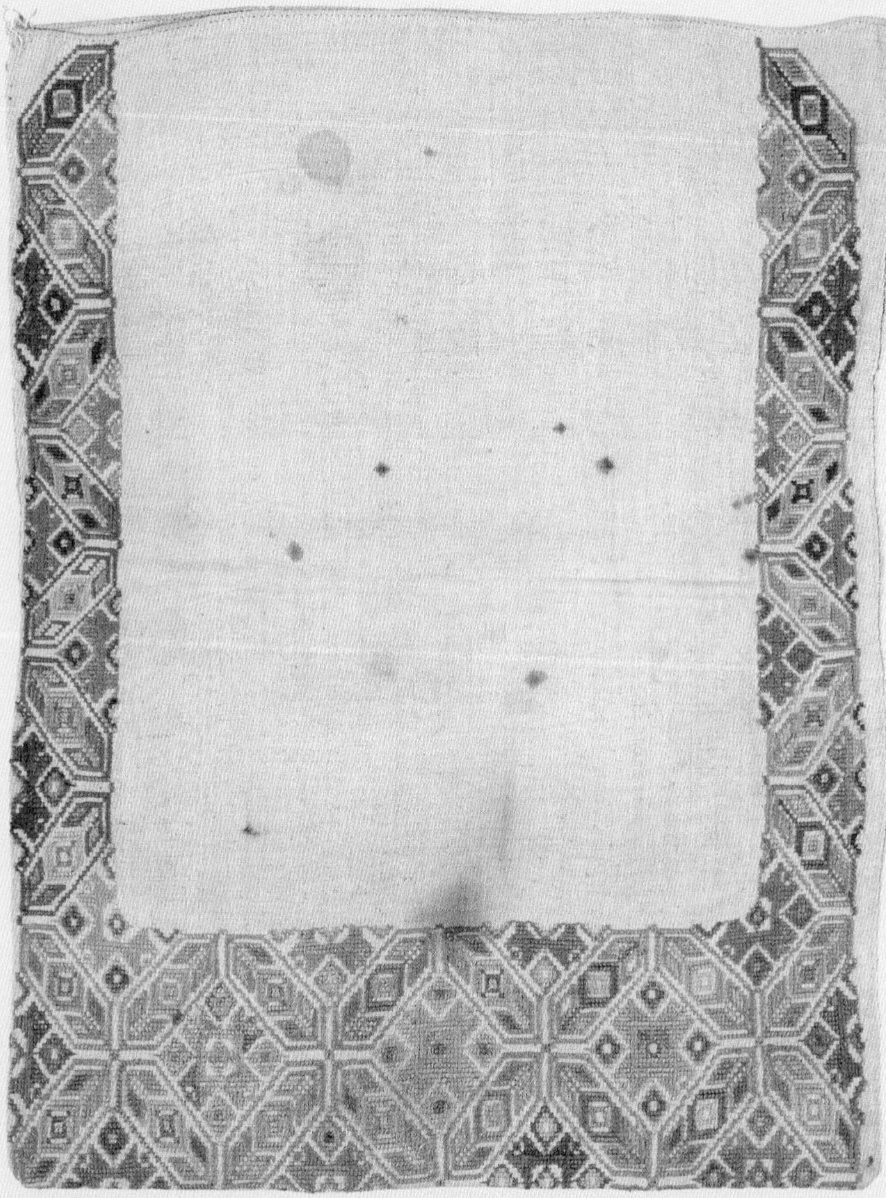

15

Cushion cover

Possibly Anafi, Cyclades, 18th century
Bequeathed by Lady Myres, 1960
Ashmolean Museum of Art and Archaeology,
University of Oxford, EA1960.114

Some cushion covers have different patterns down the sides from the ones on the end border. Here, the same formula is repeated, although halved along the sides. The main design consists of a band of saltires within diamonds, each bordered by long, hexagonal lozenges. The outlines defining each motif are created by voided lines, while the pattern itself is worked in muted coloured silks.

As with Cat. 14, one end of this cushion cover has been left undecorated, as it would not have been seen when all the cushions were stacked one above the other.

Foundation: warp: linen, undyed, off-white, Z-spun, average 18 threads per cm; weft: linen, undyed, off-white, Z-spun, average 15 threads per cm

Structure: balanced plain weave
Dimensions: 49.7 x 38 cm
Edge finish: one folded edge, two edges of seamed selvedges, one hemmed open edge

Embroidery threads: silk, Z2S, in cream, beige, yellow, orange, red, light green, dark green, grey and pale blue
Embroidery stitches: cross stitch and long-armed cross stitch

16

Fragment of a runner

Possibly Naxos, Cyclades or Italy, probably 18th century
Bequeathed by Lady Myers, 1960
Ashmolean Museum of Art and Archaeology,
University of Oxford, EA1960.154

Fig. 40 Border fragment, Italy, circa 1575-1625, silk on linen, 19 x 40.6 cm. Art Institute of Chicago, 1907.826, Art Institute of Chicago Purchase Fund

Two bird-headed creatures twist at the centre of this fragment, their scaled necks emerging from two scrolling acanthus leaves set between two borders of flowers. Known as 'grotesques', these fanciful combinations of vegetal, animal and fantastic forms were especially popular in Renaissance art, aspects of which entered Greek island design via Italianate immigrants residing in some of Venice's colonies in the Aegean.

Both the design and the embroidery technique are unlike those usually found on embroideries from the Cyclades. It is possible that the larger textile from which our fragment came was imported from Italy, or that it copied an Italian original made by Latins living in the archipelago (Fig. 40). A similar example, owned by Roderick Taylor, was dated by him to about 1720, and attributed to Latin Naxos. This may have been influenced by a related piece with a different design in the Victoria and Albert Museum, linked to the Cyclades.[31]

Foundation: warp: linen, undyed, off-white, Z-spun, average 26 threads per cm; weft: linen, undyed, off-white, Z-spun, average 26 threads per cm

Structure: balanced plain weave
Dimensions: 34 x 25.3 cm
Edge finish: edges concealed by full lining

Embroidery thread: silk, single floss, untwisted, green
Embroidery stitches: cross-stitch and button hole stitch

Comments: six joined fragments stitched together onto a backing fabric; missing areas partly filled in at a later stage to complete the design, but now faded

17

Fragment of a runner with vases and dragons

Possibly Naxos, Cyclades, or Italy, probably 18th century
Bequeathed by Lady Myres, 1960
Ashmolean Museum of Art and Archaeology,
University of Oxford, EA1960.152e

This fragment can be compared with Cat. 16 and be similarly attributed to Italy or Naxos, based on shared technical and design features. Executed in long-armed cross stitch, the design of this piece is also in reserve against the red ground, but has a different combination of animal and vegetal forms. It is centred on a waisted vessel flanked by two large gadrooned baluster urns with foliate bases and handles. Between them hang dragons with coiled bodies, whose facial features – eyes, nostrils, fangs and lolling tongues, as well as spines and scales – are depicted in impressive detail. Running along the lower edge is a line of diagonal leaves; this was probably repeated on the upper edge, which is now missing.

Foundation: warp: linen, undyed, off-white, Z-spun, average 21 threads per cm; weft: linen, undyed, off-white, Z-spun, average 21 threads per cm

Structure: balanced plain weave
Dimensions: 55 x 15.2 cm
Edge finish: one selvedge, two cut edges, one edge with traces of crochet trim

Embroidery thread: silk, single floss, untwisted, red
Embroidery stitches: long-armed cross stitch

18

Chemise skirt border

Southern Cyclades, 18th–19th century
Bequeathed by Lady Myres, 1960
Ashmolean Museum of Art and Archaeology,
University of Oxford, EA1960.124

This finely embroidered fragment is typical of the decorative borders found on Cycladic chemises. These were worn under dresses, with only the decorated areas exposed. This tubular piece comprises two full loom-widths and one cut section joined at the seams with bibila lace, also known as needle lace. The same technique is used for the trim along the hemline.

The design is condensed into a narrow band of repeating motifs executed in satin and cross-stitch, including figures with hats, possibly women. Some have square bodies, while others are rounded. They are flanked by confronting peacocks and alternate with vases of flowers and ships with square sails. This same pattern continues up the side slits, thus extending the frieze further into the plain background.

The Victoria and Albert Museum has a fragment with a similar design, but it is drawn in a slightly different manner. Once part of the collection of A. J. B. Wace, it has been tentatively attributed to the island of Kimolos.[32] A stylistic similarity with other examples associated with the nearby island of Sifnos suggests that our example, too, could be from the southern Cyclades.

Foundation: warp: cotton, undyed, off-white, Z-spun, average 18 threads per cm; weft: cotton, undyed, off-white, Z-spun, average 13 threads per cm

Structure: balanced plain weave
Dimensions: 80 x 64 cm
Edge finish: two folded edges, one cut edge, one hemmed edge

Embroidery thread: silk, untwisted, S- and Z-spun, cream, salmon-pink, red, light brown, pale blue, green
Embroidery stitches: cross-stitch, double-running stitch, satin stitch, buttonhole stitch, bibila or needle lace

19

Chemise

Dodecanese, 19th century
Presented by Mrs Burton, 1971
Ashmolean Museum of Art and Archaeology,
University of Oxford, EA1971.34

Resembling robes, chemises were generally worn by Greek women under a dress or an overskirt. As the neckline, sleeves and hem usually remained visible, these were often decorated with embroidery, which was particularly elaborate if the garment was intended for special occasions.[33] This Ashmolean example was probably one such special chemise, judging by the fine embroidery, the use of metal-wrapped thread, and its good condition.

The main body of the robe is made from a single loom-width which runs up the front, over the shoulders and down the back. At each side are two joined sections of the same fabric, but cut and tapered, with the same silk stripes that border the central panel. Coloured stitching is used to join the seams, with needle lace in alternating colours for the decorative edges at the hem, cuffs and neck.

Different needlework techniques are used for each part. The sleeves are worked in cross stitch with small posies of flowers arranged diagonally, but each within a square format, giving a slightly chequered effect. The more elaborate decoration at the hem has a repeat of the *glastra*, or flower vase. On each motif, a symmetrically arranged bouquet is centred on a lobed flower, alternately in pale blue or dark red. The flexibility of outline and satin stitch are here used to great effect to describe even the most minute botanical details on each flower, down to the tiniest pistil and petal. Beneath these vases is a secondary border of small quatrefoils in corresponding colours. Around the neck are tiny, simplified versions of the floral motifs found around the hem.

Foundation: warp: linen, undyed, off-white, Z-spun and silk, undyed and untwisted, average 18 threads per cm; weft: linen, undyed, off-white, Z-spun average 22 threads per cm

Structure: balanced plain weave

Dimensions: 137 x 154.8 cm

Embroidery thread: silk, Z2S, beige, pale orange, salmon-pink, dark pink, lime-green, olive-green, pale blue, black-brown; traces of metal thread wrapped round a silk core

Embroidery stitches: cross stitch, outline stitch, buttonhole stitch, satin stitch

20

Door section of a bed tent

Northern Dodecanese, 17th–18th century
Presented by John Buxton, 1978
Ashmolean Museum of Art and Archaeology,
University of Oxford, EA1978.101

Bedding was the ultimate symbol of women's domestic abilities and married life. It is thus no surprise that it became the focus of Greek embroiderers and the area where their skill and good taste excelled. As discussed earlier in this catalogue, the positioning of the beds at the end of single-room dwellings in certain areas of the Greek archipelago led to the development of textiles that could provide some form of privacy. Bed curtains and tents offered two alternatives, the first used for beds located in a niche or an alcove, the other for those placed on a raised platform (**Fig. 37**). In the Dodecanese, the tent was made of several tapering panels sewn together to form a bell-shaped awning fixed to an octagonal wooden plaque that hung from the ceiling. The bed was reached through a long vertical opening, or doorway, which was therefore the most elaborately decorated part.[35]

The tent section shown here includes the doorway and, although now incomplete, it still gives a sense of the effort and expense that went into the original piece.[36] The five joined panels, in various widths, form a central gabled section with tapering side walls. The inner and outer tips of the doorway are defined by narrow borders with diamond lozenges enclosing small quadrupeds, possibly lions. The empty reserves are worked with metallic thread, a pointer to the social standing of the original owner. The most intricate decoration is around the gable and in the panel above. These have a symmetrical arrangement of confronting parrots, both large and small; peacocks; double-headed eagles; multi-legged animals; and floral sprays. Among them are also female figures in skirts, with what appear to be blazing torches in their hands. They may be participants in a parade or fire dance. Nearer the top are blue sailing ships with high prows and poop decks. Their crews are on board, with even some sailors up in the rigging. The side walls have ascending repeats of the *spitha*, a V-shaped stylised tree, each of which has two confronting peacocks and more lions.

Foundation: warp: linen, undyed, off-white, Z-spun, average 17 threads per cm; weft: linen, undyed, off-white, Z-spun, average 17 threads per cm

Structure: balanced plain weave
Dimensions: 240 x 215 cm
Edge finish: one selvedge, three hemmed edges

Embroidery thread: silk, untwisted and Z2S, cream, red, light green, medium green, pale blue; metal thread wrapped around a silk core
Embroidery stitch: chain stitch, running stitch, satin stitch, long-armed cross stitch

Comments: traces of what are probably quality-control stamps in two areas[34]

21

Bed curtain

Dodecanese, 17th–18th century
Presented by John Buxton, 1978
Ashmolean Museum of Art and Archaeology,
University of Oxford, EA1978.115

The similarity of the domestic traditions in parts of both the Dodecanese and the nearby Cyclades led to the adoption of comparable types of embroidered hanging, as well as related designs. Thus, in both areas, curtains were used to adorn the marital bed, a dominant feature in island houses.

This curtain consists of three loom-widths decorated with an ascending repeat of the *glastra* motif, or flowerpot, while each section is bordered with ranks of simple squares with quatrefoils in reserve. The whole piece is worked in only two colours, a dark red and three shades of a subdued green. The latter's colour changes appear to be random and could be the result of using different batches of silk that had not been treated quite the same way during the dyeing process.

The understatement of the sparse, well-spaced decoration brings a certain stark sophistication to this curtain, but the interest of the intricate patterns is in the detail. Each of the larger motifs is a miniature cosmos and an interesting cultural mix, with its combination of motifs such as the double-headed eagle, stylised lions and tulip-carnation sequences drawing on Byzantine, Venetian and Ottoman visual parallels.

Foundation: warp: linen, undyed, off-white, Z-spun, average 15 threads per cm; weft: linen, undyed, off-white, Z-spun, average 15 threads per cm

Structure: balanced plain weave
Dimensions: 295 x 149.5 cm
Edge finish: two selvedges, two hemmed edges

Embroidery thread: silk, untwisted and S-spun, red, green
Embroidery stitch: cross stitch

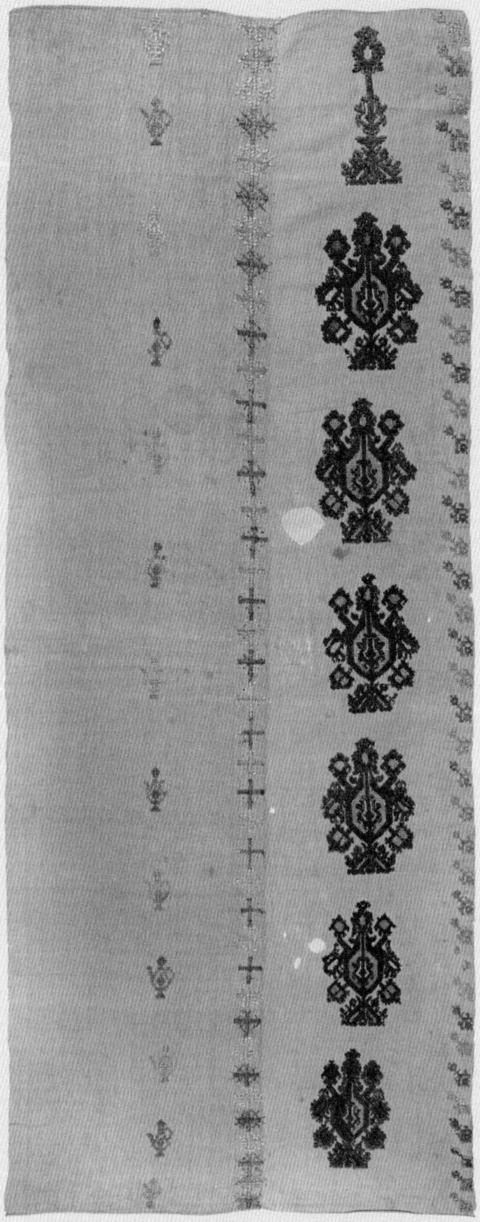

22

Panel of a bed tent

Rhodes, 18th–19th century
Bequeathed by Lady Myres, 1960
Ashmolean Museum of Art and Archaeology,
University of Oxford, EA1960.133

Foundation: warp: linen, undyed, off-white, Z-spun, average 19 (*glastra* panel) and 14 (coffee pot panel) threads per cm; weft: linen, undyed, off-white, Z-spun, average 15 (*glastra* panel) and 9 (coffee pot panel) threads per cm

Structure: balanced plain weave
Dimensions: 120.4 x 82 cm
Edge finish: two selveges, two hemmed borders

Embroidery thread: silk, Z2S, red, acid green, dark green
Embroidery stitches: Rhodian cross-stitch

Fig. 41 Bed tent (*spevéri*), with valance and cushions, Rhodes, 18th century, silk on linen. Benaki Museum, 7650

Being less visible, the back of a bed tent has less decoration than the front, as this fragment clearly shows. The right-hand panel is worked with a well-spaced ascending repeat of the *glastra*, or flowerpot, here containing rosebuds. Slightly to the left of the central seam lies a vertical repeat of small, embellished crosses, alternately in green and cream or yellow. The more spacious left-hand section is worked with a series of small coffee pots in yellow and an acidic green. The right-hand edge has a repeat of floral motifs arranged on the diagonal. The overall effect is much less crowded than on the heavily embroidered front sections of these elaborate bed tents (**Fig. 41**).

The thick and often untwisted embroidery silk produces a raised effect that is not found on examples from the northern part of the Dodecanese. This, together with a heavier-weight linen for the background, renders Rhodian embroideries quite distinct from others in the region. The actual process of creating this three-dimensional embroidery has still to be reconstructed. In particular, nobody has yet been able to discover how such thick thread could be pulled through the fabric without damaging either the silk, generally unspun, or the linen, given the thickness of the weave.

23

Cushion cover

Crete, 18th century
Presented by Mrs Angela Jaffrey, 2004; ex collection F. H. Cook
Ashmolean Museum of Art and Archaeology,
University of Oxford, EA2004.6

Foundation: main field warp: linen, undyed, off-white, Z-spun, average 20 threads per cm; main field weft: cotton, undyed, off-white, Z-spun, average 24 threads per cm; right-hand side border: warp: linen, undyed, off-white, Z-spun, average 22 threads per cm; weft: cotton, undyed, off-white, Z-spun, average 24 yarns per cm

Structure: balanced plain weave
Dimensions: 51.6 x 91.3 cm
Edge finish: four hemmed edges

Embroidery thread: silk, single untwisted strands, white, beige, yellow, burnt-orange, red, light brown, light blue, medium blue, light green, olive-green, black

Embroidery stitches: chain stitch, double-running stitch, Cretan feather stitch, laid and couched stitch, herringbone stitch, satin stitch, split stitch, French knots

Fig. 42 Woman's dress, Crete, late 17th–early 18th century, linen, cotton and silk. Benaki Museum, EE872 and 3308

The finest Greek embroidery in the Ashmolean collection, this panel bears witness to the dynamic visual language and technical dexterity of Cretan embroiderers.[37] The decoration – executed in eight different stitches, some combined on individual motifs – is inventively packed over a large central area and built around five composite groups of human, animal and vegetal forms.

The field is dominated by an elaborate central floral arrangement that includes carnations and rosebuds, which is supported by a double-headed eagle with gleaming wings and blue tongues bearing flowers. To the right is an urn flanked by green dragons, with brown stags above. From it springs a bouquet of carnations supporting a crowned mermaid with forked tail. On the left-hand side of the cover is another crowned figure, grasping floral stems entwined with dragons, and standing on a large, globular vase. The background brims with life, with peacocks and fluttering birds, lions, rabbits, more dragons, and a gentleman playing the violin with, possibly, his wife nearby.

The lower border, part of the original piece, has a repeat of mermaids, dragons, peacocks and more flowers. The top and side borders, instead, are adorned with gadrooned urns and

peacocks among luxurious scrolling foliage, some highlighted in black silk thread.

A close analysis of the cover's construction and stitching confirms that the side and top borders are later additions that were produced by embroidering sections of the same fabric as the central panel. Thus, they probably originate from the same object: a traditional Cretan female dress (**Fig. 42**).

The Cretan dress, or *poukamiso*, was more like a wide skirt with shoulder straps, gathered over the bosom then falling freely. The bottom of the skirt was usually the most decorated area, with a wide embroidered border ranging between 25 cm and 70 cm deep.[38] The skirt border section that is now part of the Ashmolean cushion cover measured about 40 cm. It was improved and filled in with a few extra animals – dogs or other quadrupeds – along the top edge when the fragment was transformed into the present cushion cover.[39] As noted earlier in this catalogue, the repurposing of family heirlooms was one of the ways in which these prized textiles were preserved and handed down once their regular production and use had ceased.[40]

24

Skirt border

Crete, 18th century
Presented by John Buxton, 1978
Ashmolean Museum of Art and Archaeology,
University of Oxford, EA1978.117

In this simplified version of the design seen on Cat. 23, the use of a single colour allows the individual motifs to stand out. The wide central section is punctuated by mermaids in their habitual pose, grasping the adjacent scrolling stems, although their coronets now resemble wide hats. Each is supported by two gape-mouthed fish, with her scaly tail extending beneath them. Between each of these sirens is a decorated globular vase holding a carnation and two floral sprays. The whole design is linked together with scrolling stems tipped with carnations and other flowers. Among them are peacocks and smaller birds, together with rabbits and other animals. The two narrow outer borders have a frieze of carnations that alternate with lappets edged with trefoils and enclosing floral motifs. Lappets of this type were very common on Italian lace, but may well have been derived from similar tabs found on textiles from Mamluk Egypt.

Most of the silk produced on Crete was exported, but the unspun surplus was dyed and used for local embroidery.[41] The worn silk on this piece suggests that black was used to darken the blue, as the mordant used for black dyes had a corrosive effect, making the fibre brittle and subject to wear.[42]

Foundation: warp: linen and cotton, undyed, buff colour, Z-spun, average 18 threads per cm; weft: linen and cotton, undyed, buff colour, Z-spun, average 20 threads per cm

Structure: balanced plain weave
Dimensions: 170 x 25 cm
Edge finish: three hemmed edges, one edge machine stitched

Embroidery thread: silk, S2Z, dark blue
Embroidery stitches: chain stitch, satin stitch, stem stitch, Cretan feather stitch, French knot

Comments: the original silk is lost in places, some repairs carried out in stranded cotton

25

Composite panel

Greece and the Balkans, 19th century
Purchased, 1971; ex collection Sir John Beazley
Ashmolean Museum of Art and Archaeology,
University of Oxford, EA1971.43

This montage of small fragments, taken from eight different objects, is quite an anthology of embroidery from the Balkans and northern parts of the Greek mainland. It has been arranged with an eye to symmetry, with the dominant red areas forming the arms of a cross.

Scholars have suggested that these panels were created to address the growing interest in Greek embroidery from foreign tourists between the late 19th and early 20th century. Small pieces were also collected by locals and acquired and assembled by dealers, some of whom actively operated in places like Salonika at the turn of the 20th century.[43]

The production of these panels has also been linked to the progressive decline of handmade products and associated crafts following the arrival of manufactured products in Greece. This piece came from the distinguished Oxford professor of Greek art and archaeology Sir John Beazley, illustrating once more the role played by British classical scholars in stimulating the early 20th-century interest in Greek textiles.[44]

Foundation: central panels: warp: linen, undyed, buff colour; weft: linen, undyed, buff colour; corner panels: warp: silk, buff colour; weft: cotton, buff colour

Structure: balanced plain weave
Dimensions: 92.8 x 83 cm

Embroidery thread: wool, Z2S and S2Z, beige, pink, red, powder blue, light blue, dark blue, olive green, dark green, light brown, dark brown; metal-wrapped cotton
Embroidery stitches: cross stitch, outline stitch, buttonhole stitch, surface darning, weft brocading

Endnotes

GREEK ISLAND EMBROIDERIES: AN OVERVIEW

1 A list of the most important British collections of this material can be found in the Appendix.

2 This chronological span follows the most authoritative studies of Greek embroidery, above all Trilling 1983; Taylor 1998; Krody 2006; Ioannou-Yannara 2006. Because of their anonymous nature and the way in which they were collected, however, Greek island embroideries remain difficult to date and attribute with certainty.

3 As in other studies, examples from the Epirus region are also included. Cf. Johnstone 1961, pp. 31–34, 52–53, pls. 4–6 and 1972, p. 87, figs. 101–02; Trilling 1983, passim; Taylor 1998, pp. 127–45; Krody 2006, pp. 91–109, cats. 5.1–5.12; Ioannou-Yannara 2006, pp. 236–41, cats. 1–15.

4 As noted by Ann French; French 2009, p. 82.

5 At the time of writing, no evidence had emerged of a larger collection of Greek embroideries in Myres's possession, nor of a sale or donation of more complete examples to other institutions. A box of twenty-five glass negatives picturing Greek embroideries exists in his archive at the Institute of Archaeology, University of Oxford, but its contents could not be examined and cross-checked due to the lockdown imposed by the Covid-19 pandemic. Research on this and additional archival material will continue once public access to archives is resumed. I am grateful to Dr Sally Crawford and Dr Katharina Ulmschneider for bringing the existence of the negatives to my attention.

6 Taylor (1998, p. 182) erroneously records that Buxton collected embroideries both in mainland Greece and the islands following his arrival to the British School of Athens in 1934. In Buxton's notebook, now in the curatorial files of the Eastern Art Department at the Ashmolean, however, we only find one reference to an object acquired in Athens in the 1930s, a runner attributed to Skyros, which does not appear to have reached the museum with the rest of the collection.

7 Dowries traditionally represented one of the key assets brought by a woman to a marriage, offsetting the cost of her upkeep and protection in her new life. As a result, her property (which included furnishings for the household) and money were often controlled by her husband or associated with him or his family's estate. However, in some cases, local legislation could grant women access to parts of the dowry without men's approval. In islands such as Corfu, for instance, embroideries featured among the few gifts a woman could leave to her descendants without asking for her husband's consent. Trilling 1983, p. 53.

8 Benaki 1965A, 1965B and 1966; Hatzimichali 1997; Lada-Minotos–Gangadis 1993; Papantoniou 1996.

9 Welters 1992.

10 See, above all, Johnstone 1961, pp. 10–12; Trilling 1983, pp. 41–49; Taylor 1998, pp. 11–23; Krody 2006, passim. For a more complete list of studies, see Krody 2006, pp. 152–53.

11 Taylor 1998, p. 11.

12 Runciman 1954, pp. 124–25.

13 The last fortresses on the outlying islands were taken by the Ottomans in 1715.

14 The duchy remained under his successors until 1383, when power passed over to the Crispi family.

15 Norwich 2003, especially chapters 11–36.

16 Textiles here were produced in a semi-industrial fashion and administrated through a corporation of different stakeholders known as the Mahona; Taylor 1998, p. 15; Ballian 2017, p. 88.

17 See, in particular, Trilling 1983, pp. 41–50; Taylor 1998, pp. 19–24; and Krody 2006, passim.

18 In other instances, Byzantine commanders accepting Venetian sovereignty were left in control; Trilling 1983, p. 42.

19 For a recent discussion of embroidery in Italian society, see Ajmar-Wollheim/Dennis 2006, pp. 61, 155–63 and 342–51.

20 Attention has been drawn in particular to the stimulus that an international network of users, including entrepreneurs, offered to the production and circulation of textile pattern books. The high demand also led to a growing range of motifs, both local and foreign, complicating over time the issue of their actual origin; Speelberg 2015, p. 6. See also Trilling 1983, pp. 28–34.

21 Krody 2006, pp. 42–43.

22 Krody 2006, pp. 32–43.

23 The possible impact of Egyptian textiles was first discussed in Trilling 1983, pp. 22–25.

24 Ashtor 1983, pp. 80–81.

25 As noted by Lisa Golombek, the Islamic world had a veritable 'textile mentality' as demonstrated by the incredibly rich terminology available in primary sources and the knowledge that users had of this material. Golombek 1988, p. 38.

26 Following centuries of state control, the industry was privatised under the Mamluk Sultan al-Nasir Muhammad ibn Qalawun (r. 1310–1341) resulting in considerable commercial and economic profit for those involved. However, by the first third of the 15th century the reduced number of active looms both in Egypt and Syria, a rise in corruption and unfair competition, and the arrival of more cheaply produced textiles from Europe caused an irreversible decline for the Mamluk textile production. This greatly impacted the economic prosperity of the Sultanate; see Mackie 1984 and Walker 2000.

27 Their role as main carriers and distributors of spices to Europe often resulted in favourable conditions, especially during Venice's rule of the Aegean. Carboni 2007, pp. 73–89.

28 Although the fragmentary state of this material makes the identification of their original context (i.e., piece of garment or household furnishing) difficult, other sources and visual evidence indicate that in this period embroidery was used to decorate shirts (collar area and neckline), trousers (hems), girdles, scarves and waistbands, as well as slippers and caps. Needlework for the home is found on fragments of pillow covers, coverlets, and cloths of different sizes. Others are from curtains used both as internal wall hangings and room dividers, with the latter similar to later Greek island equivalents. For an overview on this collection, see Ellis 2001 and http://jameelcentre.ashmolean.org/collection/7/10222/; accessed 30 March 2020.

29 Krody 2006, p. 39.

30 See the Appendix.

31 Taylor 1987 and 1998, esp. pp. 175–86.

32 French 2009; Greensted 2011B; Simpson 2015.

33 For an overview of women designers, practitioners and philanthropists associated with the Arts and Crafts Movement, see Callen 1979.

34 The exhibition in question, 'May Morris: Art and Life', was held at the William Morris Gallery in Walthamstow, London from 7 October 2017 to 28 January 2018, accompanied by a multi-authored catalogue, Mason et al. 2017, esp. pp. 58–151.

35 Above all counted thread and Berlin wool work.

36 The impact of her lecturing in the US was particularly inspiring to many local women and the American Arts and Crafts Movement. Thoreson 2012.

37 Taylor 1998, p. 175; see also the Appendix at the end of this book.

38 The remit of the school was in fact broader and encompassed areas of research such as geography, linguistics, ethnography and folklore. Smith and Kitromilides 2009, pp. 2–3.

39 For other training opportunities developed in Greece around the same time, see Greensted 2011A, esp. pp. 125–30 and 141–44.

40 Pesel's embroidery collection, amounting to over 400 examples, and her archive were bequeathed in 1947 to the University of Leeds, see the Appendix. Further details and an online catalogue are available online at http://ulita.leeds.ac.uk/major-collections/louisa-pesel-collection/.

41 For the exchanges between Pesel, Wace and Dawkins, see French 2009, p. 83 and French 2012, pp. 169–74. For more about Dawkins and Wace, see also French 2019.

42 For more details about these collections and their current repositories, see the Appendix.

43 This paralleled other philanthropic ventures established in Turkey in the early 1880s similarly designed to produce goods for export. Cluckie 2006, pp. 197-201.

44 Liberty & Co 1898.

45 Cluckie 2006, pp. 175–220; Greensted 2011A, pp. 122–23.

46 In the 1920s and 1930s, A. J. B. Wace, at the time Keeper of Textiles at the Victoria and Albert Museum, flagged a number of pieces to Beatrice Lindell Cook from this and other London shops. The collection, published by Wace in 1935, was donated to the St Louis Art Museum in the 1950s. Taylor 1998, pp. 179–80.

47 Greensted 2011A, pp. 112-13.

48 In this respect Myres was a man of his time, as he perfectly aligned with the spirit of the Arts and Crafts Movement itself and its emphasis on using the past as an inspiration for the future.

49 Ms Myres 120, fols. 2–12; Bodleian Libraries, University of Oxford.

50 Ms Myres 120, fol. 14; Bodleian Libraries, University of Oxford.

51 Between the mid-19th and the early 20th century, Classics was an entry requirement at both Oxford and Cambridge. Philhellenism also reached its peak in Britain at this time. Greensted 2011A, p. 27.

52 In 1910 Myres took up the Wykeham professorship at Oxford, a newly founded chair dedicated to the teaching of Greek history and culture. In his inaugural lecture he cited the Greek city states as 'masterpieces of society', thanks to which humanity had achieved a new maturity and real goodness. European Hellenism was viewed as the root of Western civilisation. Research into it, therefore, ultimately meant to go to the heart of what characterised his contemporary world. Myres 1910, p. 8.

53 Myres 1930. The desire to get to the 'essence' of the Greek man, ancestor of Western civilisation, had particular value in relation to contemporaneous debates about race and the notion of cultural superiority of some peoples over others. Myres's archive in the Bodleian Libraries contains several documents attesting to the growing pressures on anthropologists to assist in the process of nation-making through the study of human races. Especially interesting in this respect is the correspondence with his peers in relation to the rise of Aryanism; Ms Myres 121–22.

54 Myres 1930, p. 417. Emphasis mine.

55 At the same time, as the issue of how many items Myres collected remains open, as discussed earlier, only future research will be able to validate this hypothesis.

56 The Pitt Rivers Museum, University of Oxford, is one of the most telling examples.

57 French 2009 and 2012.

58 Wace/Dawkins 1914A, p. 49.

59 Wace/Dawkins 1914A, p. 49.

60 Wace/Dawkins 1914A, p. 50.

61 A letter from Wace to Myres recalls a conversation on the subject in 1903. French 2009, p. 81.

62 For a list of Wace and Dawkins's most notable publications and exhibitions, see Krody 2006, p. 153, and the bibliography at the end of this book.

CATALOGUE

1 Krody 2006, p. 116.

2 The region was the first to be annexed to the Ottoman Empire (1430), but was united with the rest of Greece in 1913.

3 Johnstone 1961, pp. 31–32

4 Krody 2006, p. 91.

5 A good introduction to this vibrant ceramic tradition can be found in Atasoy/Raby 1994.

6 The terms were first coined by Wace 1914, pp. xxix-xxxii.

7 As noted by Trilling 1983, pp. 23–25 and Krody 2006, p. 38. About the Mamluk influence, see pp.26-27.

8 Johnstone 1961, p. 43.

9 In addition to the border illustrated here, see two additional fragments, dated 1697 and 1726, now in the Metropolitan Museum of Art (acc. nos. 26.34.6 and 26.34.19).

10 Krody 2006, p. 21.

11 See for instance a complete dress with hem embroidery signed by Maria Papadopoula and dated 1757 now in the collection of the Victorian and Albert Museum (acc. no. T.97-1967) and illustrated in Ioannou-Yannara 2006, p. 291, cat. 140.

12 For a discussion of the impact of Byzantine motifs and iconography, see Trilling 1983, p. 19 and Taylor 1998, pp. 19–20.

13 Krody 2006, p. 18.

14 A similar cushion cover now in the collection of the Victoria and Albert Museum displays a pattern similar to the bottom section (acc. no. T.197-1950); see Johnstone 1972, p. 93, no. 112 and Ioannou-Yannara, pp. 242–43, cat. 19.

15 See a similar example in The Textile Museum, Washington, D.C. (acc. no. 81.86) published in Krody 2006, pp. 106–107, cat. 5.10.

16 The term *saz* leaf refers to the large, curved, serrated leaf used in Ottoman design, which is often combined with floral motifs.

17 See above, Cat. 3.

18 See also Krody, 2006, pp. 108–109, cat. 5.11 and 5.12. Cat. 5.12 has a patch from another embroidery with a different design, showing how even small fragments were never wasted.

19 Acc. nos. EA1960.139 and EA1960.141.

20 Johnstone 1972, pp. 21–22; Krody 2006, p. 79.

21 See, for instance, Krody 2006, pp. 34–41 and esp. cats. 2.1–2.4. Cat. 2.4 has the same design as our piece, and also retains the details in black. See also Ioannou-Yannara 2006, pp. 267–68, cat. 83.

22 For a discussion of this and related forms, see 'From the Ionian to the Dodecanese' above.

23 As noted by Krody 2006, p. 31.

24 Krody 2006, pp. 42–43.

25 The issue is explored in the introductory essay.

26 For a discussion of this and other Cycladic motifs, see 'From the Ionian to the Dodecanese' above.

27 A close parallel is in the Victoria and Albert Museum (acc. no. T.182–1950) and is discussed in Ioannou-Yannara 2006, p. 269, cat. 90.

28 Trilling 1983, pp. 32–33.

29 For valances and bedspreads with comparable decoration, see Krody 2006, pp. 56–57, cats. 2.18–2.20.

30 Several other examples are illustrated in Taylor 1998, p. 37.

31 Johnstone 1972, p. 75, no. 78.

32 Acc. no. T.674–1950, published in Ioannou-Yannara 2006, p. 266, cat. 81.

33 For such examples, see Johnstone 1972, p. 49, cat. 29 and Ioannou-Yannara 2006, p. 275, cat. 104.

34 In the Ottoman world, these would have been added by the relevant guild, or by the controller of the bazaar. They are sometimes found on Ottoman textiles, and on pieces from the Ottoman-ruled Greek islands.

35 For a discussion on alternative layout and construction, see Krody 2006, p. 63.

36 For similar versions of this gabled panel, see Krody 2006, p. 54, cat. 2.15, and Ioannou-Yannara 2006, pp. 278–79, cat. 112.

37 First published in Wace 1935, p. 65, cat. 70 and pl. XC. This is the catalogue of the collection of Mrs Beatrice Lindell Cook, widow of Frank Henry Cook, the grandson of Thomas Cook, founder of the eponymous tour company. According to Wace, this piece came 'from Madame Benaben of Algiers, who collected embroideries as models and had a school for making others for trade purposes. She added to this piece the side and top borders and also one or two animal motives, especially those with black, which are inserted in the upper edges of the main pattern.'

38 Several examples are published in Krody 2006, pp. 24–27 and Ioannou-Yannara 2006, pp. 286–92, cats. 131–43.

39 The use of black here and in the added borders, along with the glossier silks, further differentiates these areas from the main section.

40 As seen in the case of Cats. 7, 9 and 25 discussed earlier.

41 Van Steen Haywood 1983, p. 289.

42 The mordant was the chemical agent that caused the dye to take to the fibre.

43 Trilling 1983, p. 144, cat. 68.

44 For a more detailed discussion of this phenomenon, see the introductory essay.

Image credits

All images of objects from the Ashmolean Museum:
© Ashmolean Museum, University of Oxford

Fig. 3 After Sumru B. Krody, *Embroidery of the Greek Islands and Epirus Region: Harpies, Mermaids, and Tulips*. London: Scala, 2006, p.33, fig.2.2

Fig. 11 © Victoria and Albert Museum, London

Fig. 12 Image © National Museums Scotland

Fig. 13 © Royal School of Needlework

Fig. 15 Reproduced by courtesy of the School of Archaeology, University of Oxford

Fig. 16 Photograph © 2020 Museum of Fine Arts, Boston

Fig. 17 © Victoria and Albert Museum, London

Fig. 19 © 2020 Benaki Museum, Athens

Fig. 27 © Victoria and Albert Museum, London

Fig. 31 © bpk / Kunstgewerbemuseum, SMB / Georg Niedermeiser

Fig. 36 Courtesy of Kerry Taylor Auctions

Fig. 37 After A. J. B. Wace and R. M. Dawkins, 'Greek Embroideries – II: The Towns and Houses of the Archipelago', *The Burlington Magazine for Connoisseurs*, 26, 141 (Dec. 1914), p.105, fig.4

Fig. 41 © 2020 Benaki Museum, Athens

Fig. 42 © 2020 Benaki Museum, Athens

Bibliography

Ajmar-Wollheim/Dennis 2006
Marta Ajmar-Wollheim and Flora Dennis, *At Home in Renaissance Italy*. London: V&A; New York: distributed in North America by Harry N. Abrahams, 2006.

Ashtor 1983
Eliyahu Ashtor, *Levant Trade in the Later Middle Ages*. Princeton, N.J.: Princeton University Press, 1983.

Atasoy/Raby 1994
Nurhan Atasoy and Julian Raby, *Iznik: The Pottery of Ottoman Turkey*. London: Alexandria Press in association with Lawrence King, 1994.

Ballian 2017
Anna Ballian, 'From Genoa to Constantinople: The Silk Industry of Chios', in *The Mercantile Effect: Art and Exchange in the Islamicate World in the 17th and 18th Centuries*, eds. Sussan Babaie and Melanie Gibson, pp. 87–101. London: Gingko Library, 2017.

Benaki 1965A
Benaki Museum, *Epirus and Ionian Islands Embroideries*. Athens: Benaki Museum, 1965.

Benaki 1965B
Benaki Museum, *Skyros Embroideries*. Athens: Benaki Museum, 1965.

Benaki 1966
Benaki Museum, *Crete-Dodecanese-Cyclades Embroideries*. Athens: Benaki Museum, 1966.

Callen 1979
Anthea Callen, *The Angel in the Studio: Women in the Arts and Crafts Movement, 1870–1914*. London: Astragal Books, 1979.

Carboni 2007
Stefano Carboni, ed., *Venice and the Islamic World*. New York: The Metropolitan Museum of Art; New Haven and London: Yale University Press, 2007.

Cluckie 2006
Linda Cluckie, *Embroidery, Business Enterprise and Philanthropic Ventures in Nineteenth Century Britain*, DPhil diss., Sheffield, Sheffield Hallam University, 2006.

De Chaves 1999
Lila de Chaves, *Greek Lace in the Victoria and Albert Museum*. Athens: Indiktos, 1999.

Ellis 2001
Marianne Ellis, *Embroideries and Samplers from Islamic Egypt*. Oxford: Ashmolean Museum, 2001.

Ellis/Wearden 2001
Marianne Ellis and Jennifer Wearden, *Ottoman Embroideries*. London: V&A Publications, 2001.

French 2009
Ann French, 'The Greek Embroidery Collecting of R. M. Dawkins and A. J. B. Wace', *British School of Athens Studies*, vol. 17: *Scholars, Travels, Archives: Greek History and Culture through the British School at Athens* (2009), pp. 77–90.

French 2012
Ann French, 'But What Can the Museum do to Encourage Embroidery? Museums, Collectors and Embroidery', in *Hand Stitch Perspectives*, eds. A. Kettle and J. McKeating, pp. 164–75. London: Bloomsbury, 2012.

French 2019
Ann French, 'Making Connections: The Role of Archives', *HALI* 202 (2019), pp. 98–107.

Golombek 1988
Lisa Golombek, 'The Draped Universe of Islam', in *Content and Context of Visual Arts in the Islamic World*, ed. Priscilla Soucek, pp. 25–38. University Park, PA. Published for the College Art Association of America by the Pennsylvania State University Press, 1988.

Greensted 2011A
M. Greensted, 'Greek Craft Workshops and Their Links with the Arts and Crafts Movement in Britain', *The Decorative Arts Society Journal* 35 (2011), pp. 48–57.

Greensted 2011B
M. Greensted, *The Arts and Crafts Movement: Exchanges between Greece and Britain (1876–1930)*, MPhil. thesis, University of Birmingham, 2011.

Hans/Senturk/Thomsen 1995
M. Hans, C. A. Senturk and G. M. Thomsen, *The Pesel Embroideries*, exhibition catalogue. Leeds: Ars Textrina International Textile Conference, 1995.

Hatzimichali 1997
Angeliki Hatzimichali, *The Greek Folk Costume*, vol. I. Athens: Benaki Museum and Melissa Publishing House, 1977.

Ioannou-Yannara 2006
Tatiana Ioannou-Yannara, ed., *Greek Embroidery 17th–19th Century: Works of Art from the Collection of the Victoria and Albert Museum*. Athens: Angeliki Hatzimihali Foundation, 2006.

Johnstone 1961
Pauline Johnstone, *Greek Island Embroideries*. London: Alec Tiranti, 1961.

Johnstone 1972
Pauline Johnstone, *A Guide to Greek Island Embroidery*. London: H.M.S.O., 1972.

Johnstone 1985
Pauline Johnstone, *Turkish Embroideries*. London: Victoria and Albert Museum, 1985.

Kendrick/Pesel/Newberry 1921
A. F. Kendrick, L. Pesel and E. W. Newberry, *A Book of Old Embroideries*. London, Paris, New York, 1921

Kenna 2018
Margaret E. Kenna, *The Traditional Embroideries of Anafi*. Privately printed, n. p., 2018.

Krody 2000
Sumru B. Krody, *Flowers of Silk and Gold: Four Centuries of Ottoman Embroidery*. London: Merrell in association with The Textile Museum, Washington D.C., 2000.

Krody 2006
Sumru B. Krody, *Embroidery of the Greek Islands and Epirus Region: Harpies, Mermaids, and Tulips*. London: Scala, 2006.

Lada-Minotos/Gangadis 1993
Maria Lada-Minotos and Diana Gangadis, *Greek Costumes: Collection of the National Historical Museum*. Athens: Historical and Ethnological Society of Greece, 1993.

Liberty & Co 1898
Liberty & Co., *Particulars of a Unique Collection of Greek Embroideries (the work of Greek Refugees): On View at East India House... 23rd May, and following days*. London: Liberty & Co., 1898.

Mackie 1984
Louise Mackie, 'Towards an Understanding of Mamluk Silks: National and International Considerations', *Muqarnas* 2 (1984), pp. 127–46.

Mason et al. 2017
Anna Mason, Jan Marsh, Jenny Lister, Rowan Bain and Hanne Faurby, *May Morris: Arts and Crafts Designer*. London: Thames and Hudson, 2017.

Myres 1910
John L. Myres, *Greek Lands and the Greek People: An Inaugural Lecture Delivered before the University of Oxford, 11 November 1910*. Oxford: Clarendon Press, 1910.

Myres 1930
John L. Myres, *Who Were the Greeks?* Berkeley, CA: University of California Press, 1930.

Norwich 2003
John J. Norwich, *A History of Venice*. London: Penguin Books, 2003.

Papantoniou 1996
Ioanna Papantoniou, *Greek Regional Costume*. Nafplion: Peloponesian Folklore Foundation, 1996.

Papantoniou 2000
Ionna Papantoniou, *Greek Dress from Ancient Times to the Early 20th Century*. Athens: Commercial Bank of Greece, 2000.

Pesel 1907
Louisa Pesel, 'The Embroideries of the Aegean,' *The Burlington Magazine for Connoisseurs* 10, 46 (January 1907), pp. 230–39.

Pesel 1913
Louise F. Pesel, *Stitches from Eastern Embroideries, Portfolio II*. London: Percy Lund, Humphries & Company, 1913.

Polychroniadis 1980
Helen Polychroniadis, *Greek Embroideries*. Athens: The Benaki Museum, 1980.

Runciman 1954
Steven Runciman, *A History of the Crusades, vol. III: The Kingdom of Acre and the Later Crusades*. Cambridge: Cambridge University Press, 1954.

Simpson 2015
Cheryl Simpson, 'Greek Embroideries: The Early Collectors and Their Ongoing Legacy', *Modern Greek Studies*, special issue *Reading, Interpreting, Experiencing: An Inter-cultural Journey into Greek Letters*, eds. M. Tsianikas, G. Couvalis and M. Palaktsoglou (2015), pp. 186–98.

Smith/Kitromilides 2009
Michael Llewellyn Smith and Paschalis Kitromilides, 'Introduction', *British School of Athens Studies*, vol. 17: *Scholars, Travels, Archives: Greek History and Culture through the British School at Athens* (2009): pp. 1–12.

Speelberg 2015
Femke Speelberg, 'Fashion and Virtue: Textile Patterns and the Print Revolution, 1520–1620', *The Metropolitan Museum of Art Bulletin* 73, 2 (Autumn 2015), pp. 4–48.

Tankard 1956
Elaine Tankard, *Mediterranean Embroideries: Lent by Professor A. J. B. Wace*. Liverpool: Liverpool Public Museum, 1956.

Taylor 1987
Roderick R. Taylor, 'The Early Collectors', *HALI* 9, 4 (1987), pp. 36–47.

Taylor 1998
Roderick R. Taylor, *Embroidery of the Greek Islands and Epirus*. New York: Interlink Books, 1998.

Thoreson 2012
Natasha Thoreson, 'The Reluctant Reformer: May Morris' United States Lecture Tour of 1909–1910', pp. 1–9. *Textile and Politics: Textile Society of America, 13th Biennial Symposium Proceedings*. Washington, D.C.: Textile Society of America, 2012.

Trilling 1983
James Trilling, ed., *Aegean Crossroads: Greek Island Embroideries in the Textile Museum*. Washington, D.C.: The Textile Museum, 1983.

Van Steen Haywood 1983
Catherine van Steen Haywood, 'Early Cretan Embroideries from Greek Museums', *HALI* 5, 3 (1983), pp. 286–89.

Wace 1905
A. J. B. Wace, *Catalogue of a Collection of Modern Greek Embroideries Exhibited at the Fitzwilliam Museum Cambridge*. Cambridge: 1905.

Wace 1914
A. J. B. Wace, *Catalogue of a Collection of Old Embroideries of the Greek Islands and Turkey*. London: Burlington Fine Arts Club, 1914.

Wace 1935
A. J. B. Wace, *Mediterranean and Near Eastern Embroideries from the Collection of Mrs F. H. Cook*. London: Halton & Company, Ltd. 1935.

Wace/Dawkins 1914A
A. J. B. Wace and R. M. Dawkins, 'Greek Embroideries – I: Ethnography', *The Burlington Magazine for Connoisseurs*, 26, 140 (Nov. 1914), pp. 49–50.

Wace/Dawkins 1914B
A. J. B. Wace and R. M. Dawkins, 'Greek Embroideries – II: The Towns and Houses of the Archipelago', *The Burlington Magazine for Connoisseurs*, 26, 141 (Dec. 1914), pp. 99-101 and 104-107.

Walker 2000
Bethany J. Walker, 'Rethinking Mamluk Textiles', *Mamluk Studies Review* 4 (2000), pp. 167–217.

Welters 1982
Linda Welters, 'Greek Women Chemises', *Dress* 8 (1982), pp. 10–21.

Welters 1992
Linda Welters, 'Greek Folk Dress: Application of the Ethnohistorical Method', *Clothing and Textile Research Journal* 10, 3 (1992), pp. 29–35.

Appendix

This appendix gathers preliminary information concerning modern Greek embroidery holdings in eight important repositories throughout the UK. In most instances the data could not be verified in full, owing to reduced access to the objects and relevant documentation. Nevertheless, this compilation partially rectifies past inaccuracies, particularly in terms of overall numbers of objects present in each collection, establishing a more up-to-date point of reference for future research. The author is especially grateful to the curators and collection managers in charge of these holdings for their generous help and assistance with the collecting of the data during a challenging time for their institutions. Researchers are encouraged to get in touch with the individual institutions for further clarifications about the objects themselves and their provenance.

MUSEUM

ASHMOLEAN MUSEUM OF ART AND ARCHAEOLOGY, UNIVERSITY OF OXFORD

APPROXIMATE NO. OF HOLDINGS & THEIR SOURCES

The Ashmolean Museum collection of Greek island embroideries totals sixty-eight items mostly acquired before 1978. Forty-four items were bequeathed by Lady Myres on behalf of her late husband, Professor John L. Myres, in 1960; twenty-two items were subsequently gifted between 1971 and 1978 by Marjorie Buxton and John Buxton. Finally two items, previously part of the collection of Sir John Beazley and Beatrice Cook, were purchased in 1971 and 2004 respectively.

ADDITIONAL DOCUMENTATION (ARCHIVES, ONLINE COLLECTIONS, ETC.)

https://collections.ashmolean.org/collection/collection-online

LITERATURE

Wace 1935; Taylor 1987; Taylor 1998; French 2009; Kenna 2018

MUSEUM

FITZWILLIAM MUSEUM, UNIVERSITY OF CAMBRIDGE

APPROXIMATE NO. OF HOLDINGS & THEIR SOURCES

The Fitzwilliam Museum collection of Greek island embroideries contains an estimated total of seventy-eight items which were acquired mainly through gifts and bequests. The material is still being researched and conserved, so the exact number of the museum's holdings in this area remains to be confirmed.

Forty-four items were offered by Baron George de Menasce between 1946 and 1950, followed by a bequest of twenty-four fragments by Sir Augustus and Lady Daniel in 1949. Several individual donations reached the museum afterwards, including those by the Friends of the Fitzwilliam (1948); Mrs Wickham Steed (1953); Sir Robert Hyde-Greg KCMG (1954); Mr N. M. Daniel (1964); Mrs Gertrude Caton Thompson (1982); and Mr and Mrs George Woodbridge (1997). Finally, two textiles were acquired for the collection in 1993 and 1997 respectively.

ADDITIONAL DOCUMENTATION (ARCHIVES, ONLINE COLLECTIONS, ETC.)

https://www.fitzmuseum.cam.ac.uk/collections/textiles

LITERATURE

Wace 1905; Johnstone 1961; Taylor 1987 and 1998

MUSEUM

LEEDS UNIVERSITY MUSEUM

APPROXIMATE NO. OF HOLDINGS & THEIR SOURCES

The Leeds University Museum collection of Greek island embroideries consists of 116 items bequeathed by Louisa Pesel in 1947, along with the rest of her world embroidery collection comprising over 400 fragments. An important archive of notebooks, sketches, photographs and embroidery samples documenting Pesel's research is also part of the collection and is available to researchers.

ADDITIONAL DOCUMENTATION (ARCHIVES, ONLINE COLLECTIONS, ETC.)

http://ulita.leeds.ac.uk/major-collections/louisa-pesel-collection/
http://emuseum.leeds.ac.uk/view/objects/asitem/items$0040:1979

LITERATURE

Hans/Senturk/Thomsen 1995; French 2012

MUSEUM

LIVERPOOL ART MUSEUM

APPROXIMATE NO. OF HOLDINGS & THEIR SOURCES

The Liverpool Art Museum collection of Greek island embroideries contains over 300 items purchased from A. J. B. Wace in 1956. The collection is subject to ongoing research based both on the objects and the rich archival material documenting Wace's research activities. Relevant correspondence can also be found at the University of Oxford and Cambridge University.

ADDITIONAL DOCUMENTATION (ARCHIVES, ONLINE COLLECTIONS, ETC.)

Liverpool Museum Archives
Pembroke College Special Collections and Faculty of Classics Archive; Emmanuel College Library, University of Cambridge
J. L. Myres Archives at the Bodleian Library; R. W. Dawkins Archive at the Taylorian Institute, University of Oxford
Wace Family Archives

LITERATURE

Wace 1905 and 1914; Tankard 1956; Johnstone 1961; Taylor 1987 and 1998; Krody 2006; French 2012 and 2019

MUSEUM

TYNE & WEAR ARCHIVE AND MUSEUMS, NEWCASTLE

APPROXIMATE NO. OF HOLDINGS & THEIR SOURCES

In 1945 Robert Carr Bosanquet bequeathed about seventy Greek island embroideries to the Newcastle University Museum. At some point, this material was allegedly transferred to the Newcastle Museum, later renamed the Tyne & Wear Archives and Museums. Unfortunately, the current location of these holdings could not be confirmed by the staff at Tyne & Wear at the time of writing, owing to limited access to the collections during the 2020 Covid-19 pandemic.

ADDITIONAL DOCUMENTATION (ARCHIVES, ONLINE COLLECTIONS, ETC.)

Archive of the British School of Athens

LITERATURE

Wace 1914; Taylor 1998

MUSEUM

NATIONAL MUSEUMS OF SCOTLAND, EDINBURGH

APPROXIMATE NO. OF HOLDINGS & THEIR SOURCES

The National Museums of Scotland collection of Greek island embroideries contains a total of fifty-six items acquired between 1877 and 1976, either through gift or purchase, from the following individuals and sources: Frederic Wix (1887); W. Paton (1887); J. Souhaini, London (1914); Sir Robert Rowand Anderson (1921); Miss Teague (1927); Miss Janie Allan (1946); Mrs David Callender (1948); Miss Beatrice Danford (1951); Clark Hutchison Family (1960); Needlework Development Scheme (1962); Mrs Zoe Manuel (1974); Mrs R. D. Hotchkis (1975); Lady Younger (1975); and Susana Bacharach, London (1976).

ADDITIONAL DOCUMENTATION (ARCHIVES, ONLINE COLLECTIONS, ETC.)

https://www.nms.ac.uk/explore-our-collections/search-our-collections/

LITERATURE

Wace 1914; Taylor 1998

MUSEUM

VICTORIA AND ALBERT MUSEUM, LONDON

APPROXIMATE NO. OF HOLDINGS & THEIR SOURCES

The Victoria and Albert Museum houses the most extensive collection of Greek island embroideries in the country. The objects were acquired as early as 1876, chiefly through bequests and occasional purchases.

The most important donations include: 160 items from Thomas Sandwith (1876); three costumes from Theodore Bent (1886), sixty-two items from A. J. B. Wace (1919), thirteen fragments from W. Bateson (1926), and some 700 fragments and objects from Professor R. M. Dawkins (1950). Individual gifts from prominent embroiderers include items from Louisa Pesel (1912) and William Morris (through his daughter, May Morris, 1939).

ADDITIONAL DOCUMENTATION (ARCHIVES, ONLINE COLLECTIONS, ETC.)

R. W. Dawkins Archives, Taylorian Institute, University of Oxford
V&A archives
https://www.vam.ac.uk/collections/embroidery
https://collections.vam.ac.uk

LITERATURE

Wace 1905; Wace 1914; Pesel 1907 and 1913; Kendrick/Pesel/Newberry 1921; Johnstone 1961 and 1972; Trilling 1983; Taylor 1998; De Chaves 1999; Krody 2006; Ioannou-Yannara 2006

MUSEUM

WHITWORTH ART GALLERY, UNIVERSITY OF MANCHESTER

APPROXIMATE NO. OF HOLDINGS & THEIR SOURCES

The Whitworth Art Gallery at the University of Manchester owns some fifty-six examples of Greek island embroideries. The core group was bequeathed by Professor Percy Newberry and Mrs Newberry in 1949, followed by further donations until 1967 by Mrs Tillyard, Sir Joseph Cocksey Lee, Lady Daniel, and Jocelyn Morton. In 2000 three-dozen works with an uncertain attribution to Greece or Turkey were also accessioned.

ADDITIONAL DOCUMENTATION (ARCHIVES, ONLINE COLLECTIONS, ETC.)

https://www.whitworth.manchester.ac.uk/collection/ourcollection/textilecollection/

LITERATURE

Wace 1914; Kendrick/Pesel/Newberry 1921; Taylor 1998; French 2012